Praise for *Capitalists Arise!*

"In this valuable and well-written book, Peter Georgescu explores the erosion of the American Dream and the societal impacts of growing economic inequality. Fortunately, he is an optimist and presents a compelling case for what the private sector can do to simultaneously advance the interests of both workers and shareholders. Unlike many books about the future of our economy, this is one you should buy—*and actually read*."

—Jason Grumet, President, Bipartisan Policy Center

"Peter Georgescu, one of America's leading business thinkers, has issued a sharp warning to his fellow capitalists: they've become the unwitting enemy of the free-market system they claim to love. By elevating share prices over the welfare of the workers and consumers who buy their products, they're in danger of driving our great, corporate profit-making engine into the ground. This book talks frankly to blinkered titans who have hijacked the system. To keep capitalism alive, he tells them, all Americans have to thrive."

—Jane Bryant Quinn, author of *How to Make Your Money Last*

"*Capitalists Arise!* highlights the perilous human cost of opportunity inequality and how it threatens the entire American system. Georgescu offers a critique of how the philosophy of shareholder primacy, since the 1980s, has contributed to shrinking opportunity for most Americans. Importantly, he points to solutions business and the nation need with great urgency."

—Raymond D. Horton, Professor of Ethics and Governance, Columbia Business School

"Peter Georgescu is a great storyteller. In his new book he takes on one of the driving stories of our time—income inequality. He makes you not just understand but feel the consequences in human terms. And then he goes on to offer real-world solutions. This book will not just make you think; it will drive you to action."

—Shelly Lazarus, Chairman Emeritus, Ogilvy & Mather, and Board Member, General Electric, Blackstone Group, and Merck

"*Capitalists Arise!* is a powerful call to action for the business community to address the rapid rise in inequalities of income, wealth, and opportunity witnessed over recent years. The work of the OECD has underlined, with greater clarity than ever before, the true nature of the threat posed by soaring inequalities to growth, political stability, and the very existence of our future prosperity. Business may have contributed to the problem, but it can also be a key part of the solution. Georgescu's message is simple: business cannot serve one master alone—the shareholder. Rather, he asserts that, for its own benefit, the business community must treat their employees, their companies, and their communities more fairly. Inclusive growth is the only viable socioeconomic solution for our times. *Capitalists Arise!* is a must-read."

   —Angel Gurría, Secretary-General, Organisation for Economic Co-operation and Development

"*Capitalists Arise!* is the most compelling book I have read about the disastrous effects of ever-widening income inequality in America since Charles Murray's *Coming Apart*. It offers compelling solutions for an America on the brink."

   —Pamela Carlton, President, Springboard

CAPITALISTS, ARISE!

Capitalists, ARISE!

END ECONOMIC INEQUALITY, GROW THE MIDDLE CLASS, HEAL THE NATION

PETER GEORGESCU
with **David Dorsey**

BK

Berrett–Koehler Publishers, Inc.
a BK Currents book

BERRETT-KOEHLER PUBLISHERS, INC.

1333 Broadway, Suite 1000, Oakland, CA 94612-1921

Tel: (510) 817-2277   Fax: (510) 817-2278   www.bkconnection.com

ORDERING INFORMATION

QUANTITY SALES. Special discounts are available on quantity purchases by corporations, associations, and others. For details, contact the "Special Sales Department" at the Berrett-Koehler address above.

INDIVIDUAL SALES. Berrett-Koehler publications are available through most bookstores. They can also be ordered directly from Berrett-Koehler:

Tel: (800) 929-2929; Fax: (802) 864-7626; www.bkconnection.com

ORDERS FOR COLLEGE TEXTBOOK/COURSE ADOPTION USE. Please contact Berrett-Koehler: Tel: (800) 929-2929; Fax: (802) 864-7626.

Orders by U.S. trade bookstores and wholesalers. Please contact Ingram Publisher Services, Tel: (800) 509-4887; Fax: (800) 838-1149; E-mail: customer.service@ingrampublisherservices.com; or visit www.ingrampublisherservices.com/Ordering for details about electronic ordering.

Berrett-Koehler and the BK logo are registered trademarks of Berrett-Koehler Publishers, Inc.

Printed in the United States of America

Berrett-Koehler books are printed on long-lasting acid-free paper. When it is available, we choose paper that has been manufactured by environmentally responsible processes. These may include using trees grown in sustainable forests, incorporating recycled paper, minimizing chlorine in bleaching, or recycling the energy produced at the paper mill.

LIBRARY OF CONGRESS CATALOGING-IN-PUBLICATION DATA

Names: Georgescu, Peter, author. | Dorsey, David, 1952- author.
Title: Capitalists, arise : end wealth inequality, grow the middle class, heal the nation / by Peter Georgescu, with David Dorsey.
Description: First edition. | Oakland, CA : Berrett-Koehler Publishers, [2017] | Includes bibliographical references.
Identifiers: LCCN 2016050070 | ISBN 9781523082667 (hardcover)
Subjects: LCSH: Capitalism—United States. | Equality--United States. | United States—Economic conditions—2009-
Classification: LCC HC106.84 .G46 2017 | DDC 330.973--dc23
LC record available at https://lccn.loc.gov/2016050070

First Edition

22 21 20 19 18 17   10 9 8 7 6 5 4 3 2 1

Cover design: Brad Foltz. Book production and interior design: VJB/Scribe. Copyeditor: John Pierce. Proofreader: Nancy Bell. Indexer: Theresa Duran. Author photo: Elle Muliarchyk.

To our son Andrew
With respect and admiration

CONTENTS

INTRODUCTION

FOR THE PAST FOUR decades, capitalism has been slowly committing suicide. It's going on in plain view, although few recognize what's happening because, to most observers of the stock market, nothing looks amiss.

The stock market has become the yardstick of the nation's financial and economic health: we assume that stock prices measure the well-being of corporate and business success, and we continue to apply this metric even as the market reaches record-setting territory. Growth in the value of stocks has become an obsession. It is part of our culture. Shareholders have come to demand it. Year in and year out, quarter after quarter, profits must go up. As a result, a CEO must push earnings and stock prices skyward by whatever means possible. Do that consistently, and the CEO is richly rewarded, celebrated in the press, and applauded by the financial community. Any CEO who allows earnings and profits to languish, even temporarily, is in danger of losing his or her job. That has become our zeitgeist — deliver earnings, push up the stock price, or perish. It has the appearance of a natural, reasonable process, but it isn't. It is an unforgiving ritual, a cruel way to do business — a way through which unintended actions have disastrous long-term consequences for companies and our society in general. This is the world in which shareholders have come to demand and get maximum, short-term returns. A world where shareholders have dominion over all other stakeholders in a company. Nearly four decades of this version of capitalism have damaged the long-term viability of businesses and helped create a vast, unequal America in socioeconomic terms. Simply put, shareholder primacy has become a kind of cancer that needs to be eradicated before it destroys our way of life.

To say this within the world of business today is tantamount to pointing out, centuries ago, that the earth was actually round.

1

Shareholder primacy has become so fundamental to the way we've thought about business for nearly half a century that most of those in business are hardly more aware of it than they are of the air they breathe. Meanwhile, this philosophy has been destroying the conditions that create markets and healthy communities for the companies that make their shareholders wealthy. If that way of life collapses, profit isn't sustainable. It will disappear along with the company creating it. What makes our corporations *appear* to be strong and successful is actually undermining our entire society by eroding the ability of the general population to spend, to thrive, to hope for a better future. For the large majority of our people, the American dream has simply disappeared.

This book describes how and why shareholder primacy has become one of the major drivers of income inequality and the dearth of economic opportunity for many in America. Our economy has become a cage for the majority of Americans who have little or no chance to improve the quality of their lives, many of whom are living in a quicksand of debt. The unrest and anger that determined the outcome of the 2016 presidential election are in part the result of the destructive consequences of shareholder primacy, which has been turbocharged by the negative effects of globalization and technology.

It's no wonder that our universities are turning out generations of young Americans who believe capitalism is evil. Thomas Piketty's book *Capital in the Twenty-First Century* only reinforced this view in its central thesis that our economic system increasingly concentrates wealth within the pockets of a smaller and smaller percentage of the population — those who demand and get a disproportionately large share of the profit, rather than those who do the work that creates it. Yet, free enterprise at its best has been the lifeblood of a growing economy — the drive to innovate and work hard in order to earn a better life is what built the United States into a place where, half a century ago, nearly anyone could succeed and enjoy increasing rewards through his or her own efforts.

That hope has been all but extinguished, though not because the system of free-enterprise capitalism is inherently self-destructive. Opportunity has disappeared because free-market capitalism has been hijacked. At one time, our most successful companies felt an allegiance to a variety of stakeholders — employees, customers, the corporation itself, communities, and the nation. By operating with an imperative to strengthen all of these constituencies, our system thrived in the late 1940s through the 1970s, when America organized itself into the greatest engine of prosperity in the history of the world. In the late '70s, all that began to change. We narrowed our vision and started to focus solely on rewarding shareholders. As a result, we are now seeing in our economy and our society a loss of opportunity for all but the wealthy segment of our nation. What we desperately need now is not to abandon free-market capitalism, but to correct its vision — to restore its broader sense of responsibility to multiple stakeholders, to our society as a whole.

I'm not the first to suggest this. Many advocates for "stakeholder primacy," as it were, have been pointing toward shareholder primacy as a villain. Among others, Lynn Stout at Cornell Law School and Judith Samuelson of the Aspen Institute have been decrying this philosophy for years and pushing for a new sense of responsibility in the executive suite. Organizations such as JUST Capital have sprung up to push for a wiser form of corporate governance. Even Jack Welch, the former CEO of General Electric, has famously called shareholder primacy "the dumbest idea in the world."[1] Yet, so far, little has changed. Most business leaders protect their jobs by going along with a system that rewards them with equity, so by squeezing every last penny of profit from a firm before its next quarterly report, the executive's own compensation increases in proportion to the rise in the stock price. If they don't act for short-term gain, and instead take responsible steps to build a company with long-term viability, they fear they will be replaced. And they have legitimate reasons to fear the wrath of the financial community and a radical group of shareholder activists.

Yet they and the system that enables them fail to recognize the tremendous upside in moving away from the short-term mentality that has ruled the commercial community for nearly as long as current leaders have been in business. What's missing is a recognition in our business community of the happiest irony in this story: only by abandoning short-term shareholder primacy will a company find its path to greater profits down the road, while supporting society, helping to re-create a viable middle class, and rekindling hope in the American dream. We hope this book can serve as a manifesto for executives, directors, shareholders, and others who take steps to push back against the pressures of shareholder primacy and begin to reshape free enterprise with a vision that looks to long-term profitability rather than short-term gain. My own hope is that this book helps point the way toward that sustainable path to a future that only an enlightened capitalism will make possible. Many companies are already on the way toward it. To all the rest, we say, "Capitalism, heal thyself" — while there's still a chance. The reality is that the current shareholder-primacy model is a disaster, and it is also not sustainable. Society will soon demand change through the ballot box or in the streets. By reimagining free-market capitalism, business can help heal our economy and our society — and ensure lasting profits into the future. It is time for capitalists to arise; we need to do it now.

1.

CAPITALISM ON THE BRINK

I'M UP EARLY, READY for breakfast with an old friend, Ken Langone, who is planning to pick me up and take me to his favorite Florida haunt for a meal. I'm going to tell him how worried I am about the state of our economy. My hopes for the future depend on being able to find common ground with people like Ken: conservative, smart, and willing to recognize that our system is in trouble.

Reports regularly tell us that our economy is recovering, but I don't believe it. Certain indicators are up, but people are living in debt, and incomes have been stagnant for decades. Meanwhile, during those same years, roughly since the mid-1970s, profits and productivity have risen, with only occasional slight dips before bouncing back to the same rate of increase from year to year. What's happened over those years is that most people have been locked into their stations in life, while the corporations that employ them are thriving. Opportunities to improve and get ahead have withered, and though many people are getting by — while getting deeper into debt in the process — they are losing hope. What's needed is action from people like Ken, who have the power to influence how we do business — because business, the private sector, is what generates opportunity in a free-market capitalist system. Without the creation of new opportunities within the private sector, that profit-making system itself will come apart. If wealth rises to the highest ranks of our society without circulating back into the system in the form of wages and benefits, then spending inevitably declines or collapses.

While some celebrate how stock prices are still booming and productivity is still increasing at modest rates, the majority of

Americans feel left out and know they have less and less ability to buy the things they want and need. At some point, the choke point of this economy, the middle-class pocketbook, will quit opening. What follows won't be pretty. We need a different sense of how to do business as a whole — a way that takes into account all stakeholders, not simply those who own stock in the company.

First of all, and most importantly, employers need to raise wages. Wages would be rising already if our private sector were devoted to long-term profits rather than short-term gains. A focus on steady, long-term growth may be unheard of now in most public companies, but it was standard operating procedure for corporations in the 1950s and '60s, until we wilted in the face of foreign competition and the global economy and became obsessed with shareholder value.

Given these factors, two key questions are addressed throughout this book:

- Why doesn't the private sector see how precarious income inequality has made its profitability and seek productive solutions that both close the wealth gap and spur greater profitability?

- Can we admit that our current business model has been responsible in a major way for a crisis of inequality, and can we wake up and take action now, rather than continue doing business the way it's been done for more than four decades, until the whole system risks falling apart?

IN SEARCH OF A PARTNER

This is not an easy discussion to have in a culture where pumping up stock prices each quarter has become a cardinal rule — and keeping wages down has been one of the cornerstones of that imperative. I want a partner to help spread this heretical message, and Ken is as good a chance for that as I'll get. If you're going to begin warning people that the sky is falling, it helps to have someone with authority at your side. He's a test case for me, but also, Ken could open doors. He could persuade. I want to describe a crisis of inequality of opportunity that has grown out of business practices adopted for decades by most business leaders. It's more than unfair. *It doesn't work.* Will he recognize that?

I respect Ken. I wish he were running every company in America. His parents were blue collar, and he put in years of menial labor to see himself through Bucknell and NYU, and then he got into banking. In his early thirties, he handled the IPO for Ross Perot's Electronic Data Systems and then became an angel investor who underwrote the founding of Home Depot. A good bet, as it turned out. He dotes on that $88 billion retailer. It's his baby. You can Google his net worth if you want to know the reward he received for his instincts and hard work. He's familiar to many people in business through his appearances on CNBC, Bloomberg, Fox, and other media portals. When he endorses a presidential candidate, Ken's face appears on the Fox evening news.

I hear him honk outside. I head out and climb into his convertible, though the morning temperatures are unusually cold in Florida this year. By the time we arrive at his favorite dive, Harry and the Natives, I've pulled on my sweater, visibly shivering from the Atlantic chill. Ken probably thinks this is just another casual breakfast. I'm wondering if he'll soon be thinking, "Who is Peter to be making pronouncements about the economy and our social fabric over breakfast?"

It's a good question. I'm no academic. I'm a retired ad man and fortunate to be the former CEO and chairman of Young & Rubicam (Y&R), one of the world's largest marketing communications corporations. When I was just starting out, I was one of Don Draper's gofers in the 1960s. You know the type. The studious apprentice in the back room, consigned to research, devouring all the data Y&R routinely gathered about consumers. I learned quickly how to assemble reams of those dry numbers and stories into a picture of what middle America was thinking, feeling, and doing. When I handed it to the creative side of our shop, they crafted it into "The mind is a terrible thing to waste" or "the softer side of Sears." We made fortunes for some corporations. We made life better for others. In incremental ways, things improved all over. I was proud of what we did, even though those days are over, big time.

What exactly did we do for consumers? We plumbed their hearts and understood what they faced in their daily lives. We knew them inside and out, and we fashioned messages that spoke directly to their needs. All this worked because our data recorded what people told us they needed. Give people what they need, and life gets better. That was what drove us. And I leveraged that skill for decades, staying at the same company, rising through the ranks until I became the company's CEO and chairman.

In retirement I find myself, like Ken, trying to put my economic privilege to good use. (My wealth is extremely modest compared with Ken's, so I'm lucky to move in his circles and to consider him one of my best friends.) I realize I can't stop doing what I did when I had to earn my paycheck. I'm doing exactly the same thing — collecting reams of data, paying attention to the news, putting it together into a picture at my desk and my dining-room table, in my kitchen, in the backseat on a ride to the airport. It's a compulsion. I'm still taking the pulse of the American public, and from where I sit, the pulse is getting harder and harder to find. It's frighteningly weak.

The question is whether I can aim my skills in the opposite direction — up the income ladder toward the people who were once my clients, the people who can help revive and strengthen that pulse. I'm hoping that with Ken's help, I can reach the men and women at the top end of the economic system — the ones who once engaged me to connect with consumers.

Ken orders his egg whites with some spinach and whatever other vegetables are handy back in the galley.

"And a fried tomato. Sliced horizontally. Cup of coffee," he says, handing the waitress his menu. "So, Peter, what gives?"

Tentatively, I start my elevator speech. People are stuck. They can't move up the ladder. They don't have enough money to get by. I see it everywhere. I tell him, "I read a story about a woman who was selling her blood to pay bills."[1]

"Yep. Saw it. It isn't right."

I perk up. He listens patiently for a while longer as I go through my pitch. I tell him it's no longer possible for most people to build a better life through hard work and sensible choices. "People are carrying more and more debt."

"Peter, Peter! I get it!" he says. "You done? You got more?"

"That depends," I say, smiling. "Are you with me?"

"I get it. You're right. We have a serious problem," he says. "This is bad business. It's not sustainable. We'll get into trouble. Peter, listen. If we don't fix this, we're dead. This isn't temporary. This is structural. I've been thinking about this for months."

It's better than I expected: Ken and I are on the same page.

"We're looking at a crisis of opportunity," he says. "People have no way to move into higher-paying jobs. Wages are just barely keeping up with inflation. It didn't used to be like this. When it came to profit, used to be even the janitor got to wet his beak. Wages used to reward everybody."

"Minimum wage is impossibly low," I say.

"Right. Right. But it's way bigger than that. You get a job, there's nowhere to go. It used to be entry level, then you moved up. Now you're stuck. With no way to get more buying power out of that job. Not good. People are frustrated."

"There's no mobility."

"But listen. We need inequality. That's the thing, Peter. It's what drives people to do better. You want more. You see the kind of life somebody else has, and you go out and get it. That's what I did. I love my dad, but I wanted to do more than plumbing. He wanted the same thing for me. Fifty years ago, we had too many choices! You could get ahead in half a dozen ways. Not now. There's room to move at the top but nowhere else."

I point out that from what I was seeing, more and more people were being trapped in a downward spiral of debt, which was locking them out of a better life. People are moving down. It simply wasn't visible yet.

"The pursuit of happiness. That's the contract, Peter. Play by the rules, get ahead. But nothing better is waiting around the bend for most people. The contract is broken."

"We need to spread the word about this," I say.

"I'm listening."

This book is the outcome of what Ken and I have done since that first breakfast. It's been many months on the road for both of us, booking meetings with a long list of powerful people — the head of the Ford Foundation, CEOs of highly ranked Fortune

500 corporations, Nancy Gibbs at *Time*, the Aspen Institute, the Conference Board, and dozens of others. Together, Ken and I drafted an op-ed for the *New York Times* that got such a tsunami of response that the paper shut down the comments section after the first several thousand were posted.

OUR CRISIS DEMANDS ACTION NOW

I'm getting ahead of myself. Before Ken and I could grope toward solutions, we needed to see our current crisis as clearly as possible and to break it down into its root causes. This was to be a path of discovery. As we drove home from our breakfast, I thought of Will and Ariel Durant. I'm old school, so rather than searching the web, I went to a shelf for their book *The Lessons of History*. It was published almost half a century ago but has only grown more powerful over the decades. Their popular histories of Western civilization were founded on their awareness that cultures go through repetitive cycles over the course of many centuries.

We've been here before, to put it simply. When an inequality crisis gets too severe, it solves itself in one of two ways: society redistributes wealth through taxation, or poverty gets redistributed through revolution. But higher and higher taxes lead to stagnation and decline. Increased taxation vents the pressure of unrest and decreases inequality in a cosmetic way only for a while. It's unsustainable. Yet higher taxes are exactly what the French economist Thomas Piketty advocates in his book *Capital in the Twenty-First Century*.

The second solution leads to unpredictable and often oppressive regimes. Examples abound: the French revolution, the Bolsheviks in Russia (I lived through the consequences of Soviet oppression as a child in a forced-labor camp in Romania), China, Cuba, Venezuela, the Arab Spring, and many more.

Signs of unrest are everywhere now: the Occupy movement, the Tea Party, the angry and restless following behind Donald Trump and Bernie Sanders. These movements thrive on a sense of grievance against the injustice of our economic system. And despite the progress we've made since the civil rights era, our inner cities are in turmoil for much the same reason: a dearth of opportunity and the anger that erupts as a result. Ferguson, Cleveland, Charleston, Baltimore. Racial tension was only the most visible driver of these confrontations. Eliminate the economic deprivation of our cities, and those tensions would decline dramatically. Life without hope can lead to violent change.

Finally, the presidential primary campaign of 2016 played out the socioeconomic plight of the majority of Americans. In Donald and Bernie, the discontented found effective messengers. The consequences of that campaign will be long lasting. One hopes real solutions will emerge. One hopes potential violence will be avoided. Business and government must play their roles in the solutions, both independently and together.

But we aren't there yet. If capitalism can lift millions out of poverty around the world, as it is doing in China, India, and a host of other developing nations, it can revitalize itself here. It built the most affluent and creative middle class in history in America, a population that became the healthiest consumer market in the world. But how can we turn back the clock — or at least reset it?

We've been searching for the answer to that question. Ken and I set out to do what I'd done for decades at Young & Rubicam: draw a crisp picture of what was actually happening in the typical American household, simply to understand what we were up against. I wanted to use what we discovered to make a case for action from the private sector to find a way toward sustainable profitability by addressing growing inequality. This time, I wanted to get a fix on the average home budget and how insufficient funds might be taking a toll on it.

In much of mainstream media, talk about income inequality and the shrinking middle class has become second nature. I've been hearing it everywhere. But something has been missing in all the sound bites about America's inequalities. My sense is that decreasing opportunity is the ultimate threat to our free-enterprise system, though this hasn't been the case for much of America's history. Income inequality drives inequality of opportunity. The two are totally related. Importantly, they both share the same root causes. It started with how quickly and aggressively American businesses adapted to globalization by succumbing to pressure to move jobs offshore. Next, the business community passionately embraced technology, which eliminated even more domestic jobs. And finally, corporations moved to keep wages, except those for management, almost flat for close to forty years. All these choices have been made without a care for how they affect our society — diminishing the buying power of the American public and eventually decimating America's middle class.

Philosophically, it's not hard to ignore inequality. It's the rule in all aspects of life. We aren't born equal in any respect other than our rights as human beings and citizens. Diversity means differences, and our unique qualities as individuals derive from a variety of factors. Outcomes depend on desire and effort, a decent education, and a multitude of personal characteristics, none of which are equal. Yet certain kinds of inequality now act as a cage.

In the past, desire to move upward spurred aspiration, not frustrated envy. Lifestyles of the rich and famous were once a matter of vicarious wish fulfillment for most, not hot spots of resentment. Aspirations remained alive back then because a wealthy minority had not yet destroyed prospects for those trying to move up the ladder of opportunity. Concentrations of wealth enlivened the economy for everyone.

Now most people have become stuck. This chronic stasis was something I didn't fully understand. Ken and I needed to find hard numbers that explained the sense we both had that America was creeping toward a cliff — and maybe discover some ways to change course.

I wondered whether gross income figures alone really captured what was happening. What was happening with the average home's budget interested me more. I needed detailed data on how much actual economic freedom American people enjoyed, regardless of how much they were making. What sort of discretionary money did they have left at the end of a week, a month, a year? What were they able to accomplish with that extra cash? What picture of the future did those numbers paint? What quality of life could people now hope to achieve through years of work? Did hard work make for a better life?

I alerted Dave Dorsey, my longtime collaborator, who worked with me on my previous books, and he began studying the issue on his own as I searched for an economist to dig up and make sense of hard data. After a few false leads, I got a tip about a former staffer at the White House, an economist named Andrew Terrell. He'd been writing reports on economic issues and was breaking away from that role to start his own consulting firm. My timing was perfect. Andrew said he would gather as much information as he could immediately, and Dave, Andrew, and I set a date to get together a few weeks later at my family's summer cottage in Chautauqua, New York, during the August lecture season there. We would have a few meals, listen to a concert or a couple of lectures, go over Andrew's findings, and determine whether the three of us could bring into focus all the vague conversations about widening inequality.

As an outcome, I hoped we would recognize some actions that might help. All of this may sound like an unlikely mission for someone in my position. But in a way, this is what America is about: mere citizens stepping forward to speak out with new (or old) ideas in a way that helps. It was a big task, but I couldn't think of a better way to use the talents I'd developed in my career.

Chautauqua struck me as the perfect place to confront the facts about this country's economic plight. It was what this place was about: starting vital conversations about the most important matters among people from various social backgrounds. In a way, Chautauqua was a microcosm of what I would discover through my research about America as a whole. Once, Chautauqua attracted people from all economic backgrounds as well, but as costs and property values have risen, it's become more and more a place for the better-educated and successful elements in our society — which isn't a bad thing. The more fortunate *need* to grapple with the most pressing issues of the day, as they do here, but it saddens me to see these summer sessions priced beyond the reach of teachers and ministers, for example, who used to be this community's core constituency. But as I was to discover here, this is precisely what's happening to the entire country: more and more vital experiences and opportunities are no longer within reach for the majority of the population. Until I sat down and looked at the numbers, though,

I didn't realize how dramatically most Americans have seen their opportunities wither away.

Andrew, Dave, and I knew that the rich were getting richer, and the rest of the country was getting, well, more and more restless about it. When this subject came up, it was polarizing, and I wasn't convinced that it needed to be. There's a strident edge that creeps into the voice of someone who objects to how much money folks in the highest percentiles make. I wondered whether we could do an end run around the scolding tone and look at it from a practical perspective.

At this point, you might be thinking, "Tell me something I don't know. I'm familiar with the current economic stasis. I've heard about it, and I saw the anger over it among the followers of Bernie and Donald. What's new here?"

Well, the reality is that many of the men and women who run our most successful companies don't really believe in this crisis. They see it as a temporary lull; they believe the market will correct itself. In a way, it was puzzling that Ken and I and others had woken up to the fact that the American system itself was stalled, because the majority of the people in positions of business leadership don't see it that way. They didn't need to confront it personally. Everything in our particular set was humming along nicely. Indicators were up: stocks, for the most part; jobs (slightly); and GDP didn't look especially bad. In other words, *our* world seemed less troubled by economic stress than did other nations, and we enjoyed this prosperity. We were among the capable, lucky few who had played and won at the American free-enterprise, capitalist game. We had a right not to be ashamed of our success. Our system has always produced a privileged minority of incredibly rich people. And those who accumulated great wealth often recognized their great responsibility to the welfare of others: they started foundations, they created social movements, they advocated for change.

That's part of the dream: on any given day of the week, many can strike it rich in America and go on to do good things with that money. Traditionally, in business that meant reinvesting in value creation, jobs, and new enterprises to increase income for everyone — and ultimately create a return for investors. That's more or less the ideal, as it used to work in America. Wealth rises to the top and then, chasing more profits, gets sunk into new ventures, creating jobs and raising wages. It's a win for everyone.

Now, however, as more and more people get very rich, which used to be a sign of economic vitality, the money is no longer coming full circle. Instead, it's floating to the top without circulating back into the system. Bright white clouds of wealth amass high overhead, and still we're waiting for rain. How is this concentration of essentially stagnant wealth impacting the bulk of the American population? What might help soften the parched economic soil of most American's lives?

2.

THE DANGEROUS INEQUALITY

WE GATHERED AT OUR cottage in western New York State on a Friday afternoon, had a meal, got some sleep, and met at our dining-room table the next morning with coffee, tea, and cereal. Andrew had provided us with copies of his findings the night before, but none of us had really studied them. So Andrew took us through the charts he'd created. He's good company: still boyish but frighteningly informed, with a quick wit, wonkish black eyeglasses, and a shock of brown hair over his brow.

"Okay, gents. Income is what's at the top of our minds, so let's start there," Andrew said. "All the numbers in these charts include transfer benefits. All government support: food stamps, unemployment insurance, state and local supplemental income, and more."

He showed us a chart on how income is distributed across the American population. It confirmed what many have been saying about income inequality, so it wasn't a surprise.

"If you check this column over on the right," he said, "that's more dramatic."

It revealed the *percentage* of total personal income in the United States that each group receives. People in the top 5 percent of earning power in our country receive almost 25 percent of all personal income. The lower two-fifths of the population earn only about 17 percent of all personal income in America. Again, I'd heard this before.

Yet Andrew's next chart was something else altogether. It broke down household cash flow for ten levels of income in America: it showed immediately how well Americans are able to pay their bills and factors consumption into the economic picture. I remembered

16

that Bill Gates had zeroed in on consumption as a key indicator of the income gap in his review of Thomas Piketty's *Capital in the Twenty-First Century.*[1] He was right. Consumption tells a far more alarming story. Spending alone can be used to paint a rosier picture of our economic health — if you consider it a gauge of "consumer confidence." But, in fact, consumption numbers for households show the real crisis.

At a glance, the chart in figure 1 shows how ten income groups, from bottom to top, fare after they've paid all their monthly bills. This is simply a measure of what income arrives in the household every month, including transfer benefits (federal, state and local government assistance, Social Security, food stamps, unemployment insurance, and so on), against what monthly bills, of any kind, have to be paid, including taxes.

Here you can see that nearly 60 percent of the population stays afloat through deficit spending. In other words, to put food on the table and pay their other bills, they have to borrow money. Which is to say they aren't really afloat. They are either treading water or going down. They pay bills with credit or borrow money in some other way each month. For example, the average household in the bottom decile needs to borrow $1,386 each month to get by. They

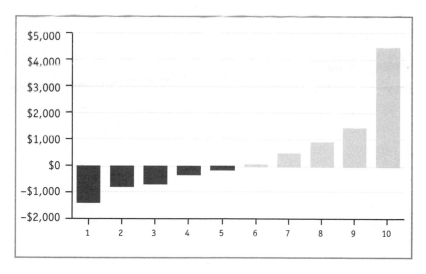

FIGURE 1: After-tax monthly surplus income by decile, 2014

get more deeply into debt each year. The bottom 10 percent find themselves in a state of inescapable debt, with the other, slightly higher earners close behind.

Let me restate what the chart shows: *nearly 60 percent of the US population — more than half of all American households — add thousands of dollars to their debt load every year.* Many of these households are headed irreversibly toward default. If they all get there, our free-enterprise capitalist system shudders to a halt. Mounting debt is the flip side of the wealth accumulation among the top 20 percent. It can lead eventually to one form of bankruptcy or another.

Andrew leaned back in his chair, letting this chart sink in. He had achieved his goal for the morning already: Dave and I were stunned.

"This isn't being reported anywhere," Dave said. "This is completely new to me."

"It's incredible," I said.

"It's all there in the data, if you take a look. But nobody is taking a look," Andrew said.

The key insight is clear. Granted, 50-plus percent of America is not poor by the standards in Africa. We don't have "extreme poverty," but we have half our population sliding *toward* insolvency. They cling to a minimum and decent standard of living, yet, in the end, to put food on the table, they need to borrow. Even if you asked people to stop spending on what they *feel* they need — to limit spending to mere survival — that would tip the economy toward recession again.

"The point is that the system is failing, and the system itself needs to be saved," I said. "You see what I mean? We've driven ourselves into this dead end, and we can't turn around. We need to push through this impasse and move forward."

"It's pretty sad," Andrew said.

"It is, but not the way you think. It's sad how the system itself isn't working. Not what these households are doing individually or as a group," I said.

"How many more years can this continue?" Dave asked.

At the current rates, the bottom tenth of the population will dig itself a staggering $15,000 deeper into debt every year. The next decile up adds more than $9,000 to its debt in that same period. The third decile from the bottom gets nearly $8,000 deeper into debt each year. At this rate, roughly a third of the nation's households will eventually default. Not only can these households not save or invest, they are clinging to whatever they have by using whatever is left of their lines of credit, or by falling back on usurious loans.

You could argue that this snapshot includes people who have temporarily lost income between jobs or have taken on debt they will pay back quickly in succeeding years — skewing the figures. Yet the way to look at this data is the way you look at a balance sheet for a company. It's a static picture at one point in time, even though individuals are constantly moving in and out of these deciles as their job situation and personal income fluctuate. Some people find ways to pay their debts with the help of family and friends; some rely on charity or philanthropic assistance. Not everyone who is underwater at this moment will default on his or her debts. Individuals may move up or down in the economic strata, certainly, but the overall picture — the larger reality itself — remains the same.

The reality is that just over half of American households are technically insolvent. They are at risk of sinking deeper into debt every year on a path that too often leads to personal bankruptcy. And even if it doesn't, they can't spend and make a significant contribution to the need for growth in our economy. A major health issue, a transmission breaks down in a diligently paid-off car, a second child is born, requiring a college fund — and they are set back in ways they can't make up. As Janet Yellen pointed out in a recent speech: "An unexpected expense of just $400 would prompt the majority of American households to borrow money, sell something, or simply not pay at all."[2]

There is another serious outcome. Being poor is actually very expensive. It's economic quicksand. The compound interest rates these folks must pay to borrow enough to keep up can range from 100 to 400 percent per year. Tragically, this rapidly multiplies their debt and sinks them even more deeply underwater. So the data is clear. In fact, America has ceased to have a viable middle class.

And it gets worse. If you averaged the sixth and seventh deciles, you would be talking about what we have left of an upper middle class. Right now, that group is hardly what it used to be. A few decades ago, these deciles would have been set for life. They would own two good cars, put their kids into private schools from kindergarten through grad school, and likely have a cottage on a lake or the ocean. Yet today, the "upper middle class" has an average annual household surplus of around $8,500. Even if these families saved that surplus, where would it get them? It's been established that four out of every five Americans will at some point sink beneath the poverty line throughout their lifetimes.[3] This chart supports that claim. Except for the top 20 percent, almost no one has the ability to save; almost no one has an emergency fund for an unexpected drain on the budget.

Step back and think about what this means in terms of the core American pursuit of happiness, which was first proposed by Thomas Jefferson as the pursuit of "property." The rising level of household debt is a key indicator of the most dangerous problem in American life: the lack of upward social mobility. In other words, it's nearly impossible now for someone here to repeat what F. Scott Fitzgerald's protagonist Jay Gatsby did during the Gilded Age — rise from the bottom to the top of the economic ladder.

Figure 2 shows how America fares compared with other major countries of the developed world in the Great Gatsby Curve, unveiled by Alan Krueger in 2012, not long after he became chairman of the White House Council of Economic Advisers.[4] The Gini coefficient indicates the intensity of economic inequality in a given nation, and the chart shows how this correlates with a lack of social mobility from one generation to the next. One can only imagine how the immobility has intensified since 2010.

Four decades ago, America offered the greatest social mobility in the world. Now, it's bringing up the rear of the developed nations. People now have few chances to move up the social ladder. Put simply: we have become the Land of Lost Opportunity.

Aside from the debt figures, this measure is probably the most troubling for our economic pulse: it shows in stark terms that the core American hope for a better life based on individual initiative is

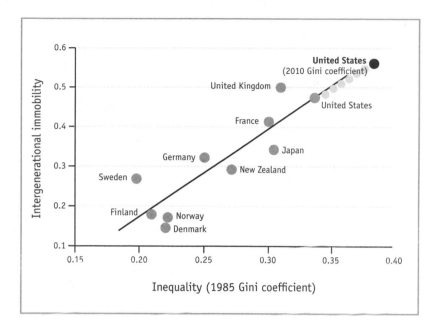

FIGURE 2: The Great Gatsby Curve of social immobility for several developed nations

on life support. The vertical axis in the Great Gatsby Curve shows social immobility from one generation to the next: the likelihood that someone born into an economic stratum will remain there for a generation. The higher the number, the greater the likelihood of remaining in place without being able to move up. The net reality, as the chart shows, is that we rank highest for immobility and inequality, which is exactly the opposite of what America is supposed to offer its people, and the opposite of what America provided at its best.

The media has been focusing more and more on the issue of the gross income gap and the national debt (not the debt incurred by individuals); yet the public and even some business leaders still have only a vague notion of how imbalanced wealth is, as the next series of charts demonstrate.

Based on a study in 2011 by researchers at Harvard Business School and Duke University, figure 3 shows what people think is the ideal share of wealth among the American adult population.

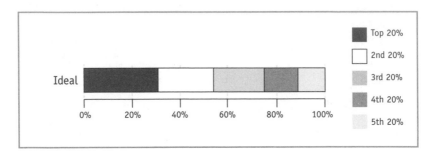

FIGURE 3: The assumed ideal is that the top 20 percent should own 30 percent of wealth

The first bar at the left indicates what most think should be the ideal share for the top 20 percent.

From the same study, figure 4 shows how most people imagine wealth is *actually* apportioned by income group. They understand that in today's world, wealth is distributed in a less-than-ideal fashion.

And figure 5 shows the actual reality, which comes as a real shock to most people.

As I mentioned, in America, the gap between rich and poor wasn't a problem in the recent past. So why worry now? If you step back, it comes into focus. On a global basis, the world has made extraordinary strides in reducing poverty. This has been a phenomenal accomplishment for humankind — and for free-market capitalism, which has driven the rise in the quality of life almost everywhere. Think of what capitalism has done to transform life

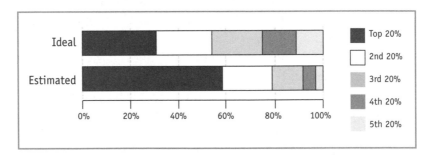

FIGURE 4: People believe that the top 20 percent own almost 60 percent of wealth

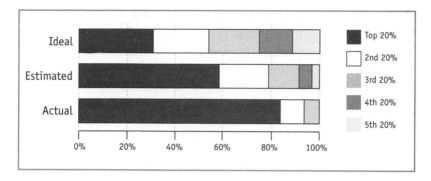

FIGURE 5: The top 20 percent actually have more than 80 percent of wealth

for the populations of China, India, Brazil, and so many other developing countries.

But for us here in America, at the moment, this engine has slowed to a crawl. This extraordinary creator of wealth — free-market capitalism — isn't working for anyone but the people at the very top. In times past, it offered the rest of the world a beacon of hope for a better life. It built the strongest, most affluent middle class in world history. We boasted the world's strongest economy and military. The most urgent question we face now is why we no longer play those roles.

✳✳✳

The emerging poor represent a larger and larger portion of our citizenry. The problem is not North vs. South or East vs. West; within our borders, rich and poor are woven together throughout nearly every city and county now. The invisible Poor Next Door can have an address in an upper-middle-class neighborhood, but they won't be keeping it. Their net worth may have been nullified already, in real terms, as many are still living in their "underwater" homes — where the mortgage exceeds the home's value — by virtue of their underwater budgets.

It's a politically and socially explosive juxtaposition of a losing economic struggle for many in a country that publicizes, through advertising and entertainment, how the lucky few are still realizing their dreams. Watch Jennifer Aniston in her commercial for Emirates Airlines, waking from a "nightmare" of flying in a jet that doesn't have a bar and a shower for her.[5] Anyone with a television can feel the taunt embedded in that commercial — when was the last time you, mere commoner, took a shower at 30,000 feet?

The Brookings Institution found that income inequality rises in the most economically vital cities, such as New York and San Francisco. In other words, the greater the income *growth*, the greater the *inequality*.[6] The growth is all at the top. *And this is where diverse zip codes are packed most closely together.* There are clear sight lines between the richest and their neighbors who may be living at the edge of solvency. In those cities, the gap is everywhere visible to those who are struggling simply to stay off the street.

Most people in this country, with or without justification, feel they are being left behind. That top layer of earners is now claiming a slightly higher percentage of the nation's income than it did in 1927. (Note the date. While the parallel may not show a causal link between income inequality and the likelihood of a market collapse, the similarity between that time and our own is troubling.)

The Economic Policy Institute reports that during the past three decades, CEO pay has been growing 231 times faster than the average worker's salary.[7] Compensation in the executive suite grew 725 percent in that period, while a typical worker's wage rose only 17 percent. Some CEO pay is a multiple of a thousand more than the average wage.

Here is the most dramatic "number behind the numbers": the Bureau of Labor Statistics has shown that the number of unemployed Americans age sixteen and older — those who want to work but can't find a job — is an eye-popping 92 million. The only numbers you tend to hear about are the so-called unemployment numbers. The 9.5 million Americans considered unemployed are those who are actively seeking work but not finding it. That's all. They represent around 5 percent of the 156 million who are considered able participants in the labor force, who are either employed or looking for employment. *These numbers completely obscure the enormous level of structural unemployment.* Put another way, only 63 percent of those able to work actually have a job or are looking

for one — *a third of the employable population is out of work.*
With only a modicum of training, a good many of that structurally unemployed third of the population could well be engaged in
some economically productive activity.

So far, we have discussed the tragic reality of income inequality. But the real impact on society is what income inequality helps
to produce. The real inequality that results from this income dis-
parity is the resultant inequality of opportunity. That is the human
tragedy in America today. I hope the pages that follow show the
link between income inequality and the loss of opportunity, the
loss of hope, and the loss of the American dream. These are a serious threat to our democracy and our way of life.

3.

THE OUTCOME OF INEQUALITY

It is often claimed that there is much tolerance in the U.S. for high levels of inequality as long as that inequality arises from a fair contest in which all children, no matter how poor or rich their parents, have the same opportunities to get ahead.

—Miles Corak, Canadian economist[1]

WHEN KEN LANGONE AND I talk to business leaders, we encounter what to us is a strange reaction from many of them. They want to know why we're wedging issues of inequality of opportunity and income into the business arena. They see it essentially as something outside their field: their job is to make a profit and grow the business, not to be a steward of the larger society. The fact that this country began splitting itself in two some decades ago, in part because of choices made by our public companies, hasn't crossed their minds. That's understandable. Based on today's operating philosophy, it shouldn't be their concern. They believe business leaders should simply follow what "the market" demands and succeed or fail based on nothing else. Period. We find in these conversations an insistence on a total disconnection between business and what happens in the larger social scene.

After seeing and hearing evidence of this rupture repeatedly — for months — our crisis began to seem more understandable. The people who have the power to really address it immediately — and powerfully — simply refuse to recognize that they should play that role. What's more startling is that they don't actually see the problem we're facing. They aren't aware of the growing ranks of the Poor Next Door. Also, they don't think a profit-seeking enterprise

26

is designed to help address this reality in its long-term strategy for growth. (Even though it's manifestly the biggest obstacle to growth facing the private sector.) They prefer the bubble of isolation. No distractions, no complications, please. Let's allow business to seek only its own most profitable level — as though profit has always been the one and only consideration of a business enterprise. This hasn't always been the case.

I knew at this point that I was going to have to break into the isolation chamber of the executive suite with some of the truth about what's happening outside it. We in business are, in part, culpable for the enormous crisis surrounding us. No, we didn't create the damage by ourselves, as I will describe a little later. But the lack of fair wages has had a devastating impact on the vanishing middle class. And the lack of serious investment in our businesses, in the creative research and development (R&D) that ensures a better future, has eroded our job base.

Business leaders are first of all citizens of their native country, which in the case of the United States has bestowed plentiful tax breaks that encourage growth, profit, and loyalty when it comes time to locate production facilities. When the question of higher wages comes up, why are we unable to link a business, and its everhigher profits, with the people and the communities that help create those profits? The absence of that simple, clear, and obvious link has done untold harm; it has split the country apart — and has darkened the future potential of the private sector itself.

OUR CHARTS BECOME FLESH AND BLOOD

After we finished with our conference on the charts, I took a walk down through the Chautauqua Institution village toward the amphitheater. My mind drifted toward memories of a conversation I'd had with Robert Putnam, author of *Bowling Alone*, a brilliant book about the collapse of communities in America.[2] As it happened, he was in Chautauqua to give a public lecture that week based on his latest book, *Our Kids*, about inequality in America.

When I got back, we convened again, and I told Andrew and Dave that I'd spent the past hour thinking about how my conversation with Putnam, as well as his lecture, confirmed the consequences of the numbers we'd been discussing earlier. As well as anyone, Putnam knew how to put flesh and blood on the issue of inequality of opportunity.

In his lecture and in our casual conversation, he had said that people weren't aware of how precarious the country's situation is, and we agreed that we saw this in our own circle of acquaintances. To be honest, I was a little startled that somebody who had gone to Oxford would be seeing the impact of inequality among people he knew.

He elaborated on some of what he'd said in his talk at the amphitheater, a story about his granddaughter, Miriam, whose parents had the privilege of attending Harvard, and Miriam had attended an equally prestigious university as well. One would assume that his granddaughter had a good future. There's a reason for that. He'd grown up in Port Clinton, Ohio, which was not a thriving corner of the economy, but he was lucky enough to get into good schools. This wasn't true of many of his friends in high school. One of them, Joe, didn't go to college after graduation. He became a firefighter.

It was one of the only paths available to his friend. Putnam talked about how the factories had shut down in Ohio, how the Rust Belt had declined, and how Cleveland had lost jobs and industries, along with the rest of America, to offshore suppliers. Prospects for a better future evaporated along with those jobs.

Joe has a granddaughter, too: Mary Sue. Her parents were never able to find steady jobs after industry moved out. Her parents split up, and her mother became a pole dancer.

I asked Robert whether he had been close with Joe as a youth. Yes, he had. But their lives couldn't have turned out in more dramatically different ways. Joe's granddaughter was physically abused and neglected. She described having a yellow mouse as a companion in their trailer. That was her sole, regular companionship.

It sounded like the movie *Room*.

Now she was grown and had moved beyond that squalor and had a boyfriend. She claimed she could find a job as a model in Toledo. I suspected I knew what that meant. She was the same age as Putnam's granddaughter Miriam. Putnam and Joe were close friends, from the same town; yet because of the growing opportunity gap, their progeny couldn't have been further apart.

He said it was simply indicative of what was happening to the economy as a whole.

As I got to this point, recounting the conversation I'd had, Andrew said, "He doesn't have to tell *us*. That's what we've been looking at all morning."

"Those girls don't live in the same universe, let alone the same zip code," I said.

✷✷✷

Sitting around our dining-room table, the three of us unpacked all the ways in which our economic straits are becoming greater and greater liabilities: one thing leads to another. In his lecture, Putnam had said that this story reflects a broader, nationwide pattern that has developed over the past thirty years. What you earn determines how much time you are able to spend with your children, he pointed out. Studies have shown that those with a college degree are more likely to have family dinners together. And families that have meals together generally raise children who have higher aptitudes for learning. All of this is especially crucial in the earliest years of a child's life, but expenditures on children have an impact all the way to adulthood: summer camps, higher-quality day care, even visits to a zoo or Disney World help a child's ability to learn and grow intellectually. It's all mental stimulus that's dependent on a family's ability to earn and spend.

The Miriams of the world — growing up in families of means — have lots of people in their lives who want to help them. But that isn't the case for the Mary Sues, growing up in families without means. Increasingly, your chances in life are determined by one decision that you were never able to make — whether you would have college-educated parents or high-school educated parents. The caste you are born into is the one that almost invariably constrains you for the rest of your life.

As income has stalled and unemployment becomes structural, families are slowly falling apart. Everything conspires to keep a poor family, or a middle-class family that's merely struggling, exactly where it is. Education has declined precipitously in the zip codes where real estate doesn't generate enough tax revenue to support good schools. America is in the lowest quartile in the developed world in rankings for secondary education. Drop-out rates in those impoverished zip codes are more than 60 percent. Even those who get to college often quit because they lack adequate funds, haven't developed strong learning habits, or lack social support from family — especially if their parents haven't completed college themselves.

We've learned that two-parent households provide an advantage for children in multiple ways. More than half the less-educated, lower-income households are headed by one parent. Couples share parenting responsibilities in more than 80 percent of upper-income, highly educated households. The mother, who works more than one job to feed her kids, usually heads those single-parent families. Where are the dinner conversations in these homes? Where is the sympathetic ear for stories about trouble at school or with friends? Who has the time to simply *listen* to the children when one parent is working two shifts, especially when there is more than one child in the home? Except through her example of hard work, how is she to pass along lessons in morality and ethics?

In the past decade, science has determined that a child's brain requires formal education of some kind as early as the age of three. The brain needs organized stimulation to develop learning pathways — it accelerates learning, beginning in first grade and continuing beyond it. A child born to parents in the top quintile of income benefits from this research because those parents know about it and enroll their children accordingly in preschool. Pre-K learning centers are booming because there's a market for them among the people who can afford it. It's easy to see how this system handicaps the majority of America's school children from the very start.

Statistics show the importance of high-quality pre-K education and the consequences, years later, of its absence: drug and alcohol abuse, crime, and high unemployment — all of which create a vicious cycle of persistent poverty for children who have no access to high-quality early education. We know that the publicized 5 percent unemployment rate is a fantasy that overlooks the larger number of those who have quit looking for work. The ultimate outcome of this structural unemployment is a much lower quality of life and lower life expectancy. In fact, if you take the top 1 percent and bottom 1 percent of the income strata, the difference in the average life expectancy is fifteen years. While some of these issues may have a greater impact on African American and Latino families, the number of white Americans falling into poverty and persistent unemployment is growing fast. The death rates for Caucasian men and women has risen sharply since 2001, and it has been attributed to problems with drugs and alcohol, as well as suicide.

The hopelessness this induces in struggling families is one of the worst outcomes. They live in a constant state of worry: anxious about unpaid bills, ill health, crumbling social structures, and other issues that threaten their future — from drugs to crime. Brain science tells us that the stress of poverty alone inhibits a child's mental development and future mental capacity. Growing up in an economically and socially deprived environment inhibits learning, primarily because a poverty-laden home increases the amount of stress a child is subjected to. This affects brain development in a way that hinders cognitive skills.[3]

Studies have shown that fear and dread and tension release the hormone cortisol into the blood, which prepares the body for fight or flight. Over time, and with continuous exposure to that chemical, the brain begins to suffer cognitive impairment. Not only do the household debts get larger all on their own, the tension and conflict of hopelessness multiplies itself as the individual becomes less able to cope with it cognitively — because it slowly dampens and shuts down the brain's ability to function effectively.

Science is now capable of measuring this effect. An inability to delay gratification is one example of poverty's effect on the brain and behavior. Cortisol erodes, specifically, the area responsible for executive function in the prefrontal cortex. Ultimately, it grooves pathways into the brain that make aggressive survival behavior more likely over the long term. These pathways take priority when it's time to exercise higher decision-making functions in day-to-day behavior. The stress of debt and economic deprivation actually lowers fundamental motivation as well: it robs an individual of hope and grit, *physiologically*.

When it comes to education under these conditions, set aside questions about the syllabus for later. With kids wound up this way — coming to class in the morning without breakfast, restless and hungry and on edge — how can teachers get them to sit still and focus long enough, regardless of the curriculum? In the end, you have a vast segment of the population whose default setting is simmering anger, or at least frustration and resentment. Meanwhile, they have lost the ability to focus on the long-term requirements of higher education and therefore are even less likely to find paths to the few openings for the moderately skilled that still exist in this diminished economy.

With despair in his voice, Ken Langone has told me about scores of job applicants who desperately want to work at Home Depot yet are turned away because they cannot read, write, or count. This is happening in our country, right now. "More and more people are living on the edge and dealing with continuous stress," I told my companions at the table.

I handed them printouts of a story I'd read in Kathryn Edin's book *$2.00 a Day: Living on Almost Nothing in America*.[4] It was about a poor mother of two young girls who sold her plasma to pay bills. The family resided in Johnson City, Tennessee, where the mother had been choosing the best possible option out of all the available lines of work: drug trafficking, sex work, or off-the-books temporary labor. She had to take iron supplements to enable her blood samples to pass quality tests for donation. The story said that her husband had too many tattoos: the risk of contamination disqualified him from being a blood donor.

"Here's the thing," I said. "They were still three months behind in rent. I learned this morning that more than half the population is getting deeper into debt every month. We're heading for a big fall unless somebody does something."

Millions of Americans in what used to be the middle class are losing their battles with the banks. Foreclosure rates are staggering. And with that, whatever equity a family has disappears. Displacement of this sort is tragic, often inevitable for families who have zero wealth-generating assets. The middle class, whose spending fuels free-market capitalism, keeps getting smaller and smaller. As a result, opportunity itself becomes an elite privilege, rising increasingly to the highest levels, where social mobility isn't even needed. The end game is that Americans are locked in place, economically and socially. We have developed an economically determined caste system, much like India's social one. It's nearly impossible to escape it. There are now two simple ways to predict a child's future: the education level of the parents and the child's zip code.

Years ago I had a drink with my boss, back when I still had one. It was an opportunity to share some thoughts after having worked together for a decade. He was brilliantly creative, and he was also a good businessman. Those two qualities don't often converge, so I admired him greatly. At times, Frank (as I'll refer to him) had a hot temper, and he could be insensitive and needlessly tough on his people. But he was always thoughtful and fair with me.

On this evening, I asked how he got to be my boss. (He was only eighteen months older than I was.) He had grown up in Pittsburg. His father had worked in the steel mills, hadn't even finished high school. But Frank's destiny was to be quite different.

He went to the only high school in the area and became a great athlete. It was a good school at that, not atypical of most public schools in the 1950s and '60s. Turned out Frank was also very smart. He learned as easily as he wowed on the playing field. That high school provided another social role in town: it brought everyone together, from all income groups and cultural backgrounds. Frank said it was one of their two melting pots; the other was the church. Every young person in the area went to that high school. Every good Catholic attended the same parish. It was like this in nearly all American towns.

Sue, the girl Frank courted, came from generations of bankers. But there they were, two highly intelligent kids attracted to each other physically and intellectually. It was the most natural attraction. Not surprisingly, Sue's parents came to disapprove of Frank. Clearly, the son of a steal-mill worker wasn't fit for their daughter — he was the classic boy from the wrong side of the tracks.

Both Sue and Frank applied and got into great colleges — Frank

on scholarship to Yale, and Sue at one of the most socially accept-
able sister colleges. They stayed together as a couple throughout college. Sue's parents continued to disapprove, but the couple
eventually eloped, and some fifty-five years later the love affair is
still alive.

But those high schools and churches no longer bring together
children from such diverse economic backgrounds. Our two Americas don't mingle this way anymore. The schools are socioeconom-
ically mostly segregated. Those on the right side of the tracks have
finally managed to keep their children isolated from economic
groups other than their own. Very few of the Franks of this country
ever get to these charter or private schools — or even to the public
schools in expensive (higher-tax-paying) neighboring towns. The
top 20 percent of Americans hang together in their zip codes and
country clubs. The Franks of the other America attend the less-
funded schools we spoke about earlier. Too many of them get stuck
at that level, unless athletic talent, serious intervention, or luck get
them scholarships to good colleges.

Isolation has become a curse on these American neighborhoods. Too few of us "20 percenters" take a look across the high-
way or enter the run-down environs of those in pain, the ones who
have to borrow money to put food on the table.

I happen to be lucky. My job got me involved with an entire
cross section of America. They were, after all, our clients' customers. Most of our clients marketed to averages, age segments, education, and income. The national averages looked good enough.
Few looked at life behind the averages. I remember reading stories
about the explosion of women who entered the work force in the
1970s and '80s — by the millions. These were the women who got
good jobs, and many went to graduate business and professional
schools. All of them, including the married ones, had visions of
career progress and advancements.

Yet I recall when we went into the marketplace and conducted
ethnographic studies with these newly emancipated ladies that the
segregation hit one in the face. Most of these middle-class wives
and mothers went into the workforce because the household no
longer could keep up with the cost of living. "This Christmas, my

kids will finally have some presents under the tree. Or birthday wishes fulfilled." That was our middle class trying to simply hold on to the quality of life one income would have garnered only a couple of decades earlier.

But times were getting tougher. Jobs kept disappearing. The schools kept declining in the lower-income zip codes. It was really about isolation, about two societies — one knowing nothing of the other. But the have-less kept watching the movies and the TV shows and kept hearing the music from the country club lofting over the tracks.

Then our clients, the CEOs, had, and continue to have, their own issues. Their daily schedules are measured in minutes, and they face the pressure of competition, calls from around the globe at all hours, never-ending reports, shareholders watching their every move, and analysts lurking in the long grass. And they have their families, plus all the issues, all the challenges, and a few delights thrown in to keep everyone energized.

But isolation was, and is, the rule. The media is diverted mostly by other news: we know more about Palestinians on the West Bank than we know about the "other America." We are terrified that ten thousand Syrian families vetted by as many as seven government agencies can produce irreparable harm to our country of some 330 million people. Stories about this populate the media for weeks. We read about drunken orgies and sexual harassment at exalted private schools, and we are appropriately indignant. But we don't read about rats running loose in public schools with broken windows unrepaired in winter. And how many of us read about Ta-Nehisi Coates's struggles as a high school student in Baltimore, plotting how to get to his grandma's house in order to stay alive and avoid bodily harm from the gangs in the school.[5] It's an everyday reality that the elite in Manhattan and Washington don't experience; they know it's there, but they don't feel it. We were shocked to read about the Ferguson or Baltimore eruptions. How could they happen in our country? The question ought to have been, why aren't they happening more often?

Isolation is the rule for our business leaders. We live in a separate universe parallel to the one in which the majority of Americans struggle from day to day. One of the top financial executives in the world (his firm controls more than $1 trillion in funds) told me, "I can't change. I have a fiduciary responsibility." Of course, one knows exactly what he means — the shareholders, the market, the analysts.

But is that the extent of it? Is that sustainable? Here we have a system, a free-market capitalist system, that is cannibalizing itself. It is clearly not serving the country as a whole. The numbers show it. The election process, in which Bernie and Donald have connected viscerally with the populace, is all the evidence you need that a huge swath of America is fed up; the other America is a big part of it. Are we simply going to double down and protect a dysfunctional, broken system? Maybe that's what we'll try to do politically, but can we as wise business leaders just keep doing what has gotten us here? America is pleading for help. And the system we already have, with some shifts toward a more inclusive sense of responsibility to a wider set of stakeholders, will enable it to thrive once again. Shareholder primacy is what's holding us back. Eventually, it will destroy us. A new (and proven) way forward can bring back hope, and it can also prove that free-market capitalism remains the best economic and social system in the world.

But first, how did we get here?

4.

THE PERFECT STORM

IN MANY QUARTERS THESE days, as well as in this book, the argument against the way we do business now goes like this: Instead of focusing on maximizing shareholder value as the primary or even the only goal, those who run our corporations should balance the needs of *all* stakeholders — employees, customers, communities — and consider the long-term interest of the corporation itself and the economy as a whole.

A thriving economy is an interdependent ecology of interests. At the center of this ecology is a robust middle class, which is the source of healthy commerce and the fuel of a growing economy. Very simply, without robust wages and benefits, spending eventually dwindles and sputters as households go into austerity mode. When that happens, profits wane and drop. Without devoted employees, customers do business elsewhere. Without vital communities providing opportunities and quality education, companies can't hire the people they need. And so on, in a continuous downward spiral. It's an interlocking system in which each element depends on the health of all the others.

If this sounds radical or something like a softhearted plea that promises to dull the cutting edge of profit making, it isn't. It's the way we did business in America when the country was sitting on top of the world and when CEOs were people who took all these responsibilities seriously. We must ask ourselves: Why did we ease away from this wisdom? Why do we continue to flee from this business model and find ourselves instead in a self-destructive spiral of chasing short-term profits?

We did it as a misguided act of compensation and self-defense —

a self-defeating adaptation to changes we couldn't control as the economy became global. To understand why shareholder primacy remains so seductive even now, even as its weaknesses become more and more apparent, it makes sense to understand how we got here.

Everything seemed to converge in the 1970s in a perfect economic storm. At the time, we thought we'd hit a big speed bump. Few realized what was really happening: our economy had tipped quietly onto a downward slope that has been steepening ever since, with only illusory phases of stock-market growth. Ever since, our economic slide has been disguised by rising corporate profits and made tolerable only through government transfer payments. In this period of steady decline, we've lived through the elation of financial bubbles, only to end up in worse shape when the bubbles burst, first toward the end of the 1990s and again in 2008. Over these four destructive decades, globalization, technology, education, tax policy, and business management fed off one another, each one amplifying the economic erosion of all the others. As a result, having ignored the consequences of our choices, our engine of new opportunity has stalled. Most of the population is struggling to cling to its quality of life, while few are able to climb higher and higher.

CHASING THE LOW WAGE

We got our first post-Depression economic scare in the late 1970s. Globalization initially appeared to be a threat early in that decade, when foreign competition began to erode our markets. Corporations realized they had to become cost-effective in unfamiliar ways to compete with lower-priced foreign products, which were manufactured with dramatically lower labor costs. We all know this story.

At first we thought we could fight fire with fire. Foreign countries, our opponents, actually offered us a chance to cut our *own* labor costs by using *their* labor to make our products. Thus followed the bloodletting of jobs that once were the foundation of our postwar economy, primarily in manufacturing. Jobs have always moved around. They once migrated from north to south within our own borders. Higher-paying jobs gave ground to lower pay scales. But even those lower wages continued to sustain the domestic economy in a different region. Factory workers spent their paychecks in Georgia or Mississippi rather than New York, but it still provided an economic stimulus for America. Those wages generated tax dollars and melted out into surrounding businesses, keeping them alive. We recycled our profits through jobs and wages.

Then we started breaking down that circle of economic life. We could make a TV in China and sell it in Europe, yet those profits often remained overseas, invested outside the United States. We weren't closing the loop. Those paychecks weren't recycled back into our system to support thousands of other American businesses. This has abated only slightly in the past few years, as some manufacturing returns home, creating an encouraging trend. Yet we're still draining jobs out of this country today, with regular announcements of plant moves to Mexico and other countries. And when manufacturing does return, many jobs once done by American workers have now become automated.

We refused to succumb to protectionism, but we never bothered to solve the riddle of how to grow high-wage jobs in America — for instance, through new ventures to replace lost industries. Instead, we kept boosting profits by cutting jobs here at home. Under the continuing pressure of low-cost foreign products, we've decimated our job base and kept our wages low. That's the core of our crisis — fewer jobs and low wages — and it radiates outward into all the other forces that cluster around it.

You might think that once wages in China catch up with our pay scales, we'll reach parity, and all the jobs will stay here, right? But what's to keep the jobs from going to India or Indonesia, and once those countries achieve wage parity, moving along to Africa or Brazil? (China is investing heavily in Africa, looking ahead, knowing that this continent will become a future incubator of global business growth, both as a market and a location for services and production.) The world has a huge surplus of low-wage labor when workers in underdeveloped nations are willing to do work for much less than American workers can afford to earn.

About a decade ago, *New York Times* columnist Thomas Friedman called this the *economic flattening of the globe.* The developing world's manufacturing has caught up with us in terms of skill and quality because knowledge, equipment, capital, and labor have all become equally accessible around the planet. In effect, the power of free enterprise, which has exploited developing regions for their resources and markets, is repaying its debt to that developing world by delivering jobs and growth through our offshore production. In the meantime, our own domestic economy is wasting away.

TECHNOLOGY: LABOR WITHOUT A WAGE

Compounding this trend, and magnifying its effects, we've found other ways to replace high-wage American workers — with technology. The greater efficiency and lower costs have been irresistible.

Like outsourcing, technology is both friend and foe. It protects and grows profits, but it slowly starves the domestic economy. On the one hand, new technologies have produced astonishing job-creating industries: personal computers are one of the greatest examples, and there are countless others. Yet, at the same time, technology tends to cannibalize itself. Smartphones and the Internet made Uber possible. That's a good thing, isn't it? More jobs to go around for tens of thousands of workers, even though some may be contract workers — all jobs seem to be trending that way. Yet how many years will it take for the driverless car to put all those drivers out of work again? Electronic innovation gives a little and then takes away a lot.

These creative/destructive disruptions began long ago as digital innovations replaced mechanical ones: Kodak, Xerox, telecom, entertainment, book publishing, the music industry, and a long list of others have been decimated or severely eroded by digital alternatives to what they had always provided. Some companies bounced back to a degree, such as HP and Fuji. New digital replacements for older industries sprang up, such as Amazon and the smartphone camera; yet again, technology takes away more than it gives. MIT reports that nearly half of all jobs will be vulnerable to automation within twenty years.[1]

The marvels of contemporary medicine seem the only justification one needs for the indispensable value of science and technological advance. But it's a difficult balancing act, and technology's ability to eliminate entire categories of human labor seems far more powerful than the sort of employment generated by start-ups based on new tech. The net-net of the whole process is fewer and fewer jobs.

Jaron Lanier, who believes technology is destroying the middle class, expressed it with tweet-like brevity: "Kodak employed 140,000 people. Instagram employs 13."[2] (Ironically, Kodak invented the first digital camera sensor, yet when it recognized what was coming, it refrained from making the transition to digital in a decisive way because it knew that change would eliminate vast square miles of manufacturing assets. Either way, adapting to or ignoring the future, it knew it would lose in a big way.)

Under the pressure of these disruptions, wages have just barely kept up with inflation for four decades, while profits have continued on their robust climb. Where jobs for minorities once flourished around manufacturing centers in our cities, now job growth has migrated, along with affluent urban populations, to smaller towns and suburbs. What's been left behind is rampant unemployment and lower incomes in one city after another across the country. For example, according to a recent report, 60 percent of New York City residents cannot make ends meet if they miss a paycheck.[3] Education has been one of the most crucial victims of this income divide — which began with the erosion of our job base to foreign shores and has continued with the stasis in wage growth over the succeeding decades.

EDUCATION LAGS AND FAILS

We all know our educational standards have taken a nosedive. Why does education suffer? Largely because it's only as good as the levels of income in the region it serves. And for most, that earning power is supported only by a vibrant economy with good wages and plentiful jobs. As the income gap has grown over these decades of flatlined wages — a direct outcome of our efforts to keep growing profits without growing the middle class — an education gap has mirrored it.

The way we finance our public schools, largely through real-estate taxes, intensifies all the other problems of income inequality. Higher income provides better homes, and better homes generate more taxes, which in turn builds first-rate schools. On top of that, good public and private schools act as magnets for philanthropy, which multiplies the inequality. The best-funded schools thrive amid the most stable and affluent households, with large coffers fed by ample property tax revenue — giving children of the privileged even more advantages over children in poor districts. In poor neighborhoods, teachers often have to provide school supplies, reading books, pencils, almost anything other than the core textbooks.

I know a city teacher in Rochester, New York, who would buy pencils in bulk and continuously provide them to her second-grade students because their parents wouldn't or couldn't do it themselves. She and most of her other teachers would print books for their students clandestinely in a copier room, when the machine wasn't jammed and awaiting service. Or they would buy them out of their own pockets on eBay. The school district didn't have the funds to buy all the books teachers needed.

College admissions only intensify the divide: those who have suffered through underfunded elementary and secondary schooling will find it much harder to make it into, and through, college.

This educational crisis couldn't come at a worse time. With the decline in the need for unskilled labor here in the United States — as those unionized, high-wage manufacturing jobs have fled to the developing world — employers are increasingly demanding a higher education from their new hires. Figure 6 clearly shows the link between earnings and educational achievement.

Eduardo Porter, writing for the *New York Times*, says that the gap between the wages of a family of two college graduates and a family with high-school diplomas grew by $30,000 between 1979 and 2012.[4] That gap itself represents more than the entire annual income for a large segment of American households.

We aren't totally bereft of job openings right now, though. Thousands of good jobs for highly skilled workers remain unfilled here. Why? Insufficiently trained job applicants. You can't blame the private sector entirely for the fact that our educational system hasn't adapted curriculums to the skills required in the job market. Unlike other developed nations, such as Germany, we do not have

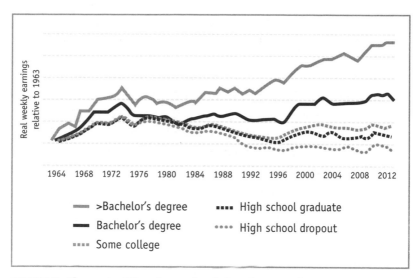

FIGURE 6: Change in US real wage levels by education for men.

a nationwide trade-school system to teach specific skills needed in our economy. We need to get there.

Worse yet, as the controversial implementation of the Common Core brings into sharp relief, we are woefully outclassed in our general educational standards when compared with other countries. The Common Core has been an effort to fast-track our kids into higher academic achievement. It was fashioned by adopting best practices from the midlevel of difficulty in the curriculums of the world's developed nations — so the backlash again underscores how far behind we've fallen. Among thirty-four developed nations (studied by the Organisation of Economic Co-operation and Development, OECD), American fifteen-year-olds placed twenty-sixth in math, seventeenth in reading, and twenty-first in science. Now we're pushing our kids to advance faster than their previous schooling allows. You can't impose high standards on a school that doesn't have the budget to implement them.

More than a century ago, we were wise enough to create public education, a system in which all children had access to standardized schooling. We were the *first* nation in the world to do this. Given our federalist system that distributes governing responsibilities, public education became the responsibility of local communities, with some additional funding from the state and some from the federal government. Parents became involved. Family life fell in step as parents created school boards and worked with teachers. For decades, it worked. Why wouldn't it? Property taxes across the board — back when wages were generous and taxes more equalized across the map — funded good schooling from top to bottom. For much of the twentieth century, the rich and the poor attended the same public high schools. In the 1980s and '90s, the rich kids migrated to charter and private schools, as the public system declined in quality. In a lecture I heard not long ago, Mark Roosevelt, then superintendent of the Pittsburg school system, spoke about how more than 15,200 independent local school boards exist in the United States, and many of them don't have nearly the funding they need to do the job — and that all stems from the erosion of the economy through globalization, technology, and the ways in which our capitalist enterprise adapted badly to these forces.

By the 1960s, our children were ranked no. 1 in math, reading, and sciences when compared with children around the world. Then, along with the economy, things began to shift. Other countries, as they began to develop economically, saw the strategic importance of education as pivotal for growth and modernization. They learned best practices from us. Many of the brightest and most talented women once went into teaching because it was one of the few challenging professions available to them. But as the two-income household became standard and women's rights took hold, many other opportunities drew ambitious women away from the field. Education began to seem less and less inviting as a career, importantly because the financial rewards were no longer there, but often because private industry offered more opportunity for innovation and advancement.

In addition, teacher unions failed to link performance and pay for teachers. Teacher unions have been tragically complacent in the failure of our public education. They totally represented the teachers' interests without linking them to measures of students' progress. Also, too often, education as a career has come to seem like a fallback choice, a profession sidelined by a culture that has come to value almost all forms of entertainment more than learning. The best and brightest talents felt no allure in the idea of going into teaching.

In effect, through such subtle shifts, first economic and then cultural, our children have been left behind, as other countries, such as South Korea and Finland, have built stellar educational systems. Finland especially guides its best and brightest college students into teaching (only those who graduate in the top 10 percent of their class can apply for teaching jobs), setting high barriers to entry for applicants and then paying those it hires very well. OECD data has suggested that some of our public and private secondary schools are considered the best in the world, but the bulk of elementary and high schools can be found in the middle or further down in the quality rankings.

At the moment, just under 40 percent of the working-age population has earned some kind of college degree. If we're to build a skilled workforce capable of creative participation in the ventures of the future, we need a far higher percentage of college graduates in the labor pool. From another angle, our educational system falls behind much of the world — as early as preschool. As I pointed out, science has confirmed that brain development often begins by the age of three. Those who are not guided and stimulated very early in life find it difficult if not impossible to catch up with those who do. Nicholas Kristof has written that only 38 percent of American three-year-olds are enrolled in educational programs.[5] Meanwhile, among the OECD's thirty-four member countries, that average is 70 percent. So, again, what does this say about America's future competitiveness in the world?

WASHINGTON TRIES TO COMPENSATE

If business can become more and more profitable, everything around the executive suite will thrive. The wealth will flow down to everyone. This is a fundamental assumption of free-enterprise capitalism. Hasn't it always worked this way? It did, for decades. And it's logical, up to a point. When the wealthiest percentiles thrive, they spend more in the shops on Main Street, so everyone sees at least a little more income. More importantly, the wealthy will want to make money with their money, so they invest in new ventures that generate new jobs. So, the thinking goes, to inspire growth at the top, we ease regulations and constraints. We create a tax code that makes it irresistible for business to stay within our shores and for business leaders to invest their earnings back into new growth. We expect those tax breaks to trickle down in the form of compensation and new jobs for everyone else — because it actually did in the golden years, after World War II. But we failed to notice how and when the world fundamentally changed, breaking down this economic circle of life.

The sea change in our economy is simple to put into words: we have the means now to create a supply of nearly everything in a way that permanently outstrips demand. The problem is that we don't see the manifold ways in which this requires us to change our business model.

Meanwhile, the government has been making it easier to ignore the urgency of recognizing and responding to this sea change. The social safety net of entitlements put in place from Franklin Roosevelt's to Lyndon Johnson's time has compensated for the way our profits have increasingly depended on wage stagnation and the offshoring of jobs. This indispensable network of transfer payments to people who desperately need them has created an illusion of economic stability. We have been able to ignore the full impact of technology and globalization because government has picked up some of the slack.

So, lulled into thinking the system is working, we've enacted entitlements for those who we expect will create jobs: the wealthy and powerful. (All the while, we rage blindly against tax increases that support entitlements for the rest of the population, unaware that they're one of the crucial things that keep the entire profit-making system operational.) Capital gains, carried interest, mortgage deductions, and tax loopholes all help. Warren Buffett maintains a lower tax rate than his executive assistant. This is *purposeful*. The shortsighted thinking behind it suggests that these breaks increase our ability to invest in new enterprise, which Buffett can do like few others, and that this will stimulate growth. But it hasn't worked that way.

Our tax structure is designed to encourage the affluent to invest in business growth. But now that public corporations have broken the self-nourishing economic cycle where profits become wages, these tax breaks merely increase the wealth of the upper percentiles, where profit diverts itself into idle pools. Meanwhile, profitable investment is beyond the reach of most people. It's a privilege the majority of the population doesn't have, as they struggle with debt, low savings, and no real access to the wealth-creating machine.

Unintended tax loopholes help corporations like General Electric, which gets to pay no taxes at all in the United States. The upside: GE keeps some of its operations here. The downside: the wealth doesn't spread out into our communities, and thus compounds our current economic crisis. In the same spirit, government continues to subsidize agricultural giants and oil companies, where profits are astonishingly high even now. While tax breaks for business have been justified as a way to encourage wage and job growth, our political system has become so inbred that the wealthy use that good-spirited willingness to create incentives to warp the tax code for purely self serving ends. Tax avoidance schemes like inversions, which move companies' headquarters overseas to avoid US tax laws, abound. And the list of other attempts to eliminate taxes proliferates.

A recent investigation uncovered how pervasive tax dodges have become:

> Dozens of major companies are using complex and secretive deals with Luxembourg to lower their tax bills... Secret tax documents reveal that companies like Disney, Koch Industries, Skype, Ikea, FedEx, and PepsiCo have funneled hundreds of millions of dollars in profits through Luxembourg subsidiaries, allowing some corporations to "effectively lower their tax bill to less than one percent of profit."[6]

All of these policies only widen the income divide, even though the general theory behind them is benign: to encourage business to thrive. Right now, though, business is simply amassing more wealth without risking it by investing in expansion, innovation, and the sort of new ventures that employ more people.

You don't need a political affiliation to work toward correcting this schism that has separated capital and productivity from any connection to job and wage growth: both liberals and conservatives are deeply concerned about it. Vlad Signorelli, of the conservative think tank Bretton Woods Research, recently pointed out, "Both Democratic and Republican parties have long since abandoned a commitment to stable . . . income growth for those at the bottom of the pyramid."[7] In truth, both business and government need to act.

The reality is that taxation and transfer payments lag behind those in most other developed nations. Steve Rattner has pointed out how, if you factor out taxation and public spending, income inequality is no worse here than it is in other nations, and is actually a little less extreme than in Britain and Germany.[8] Yet, once you factor in tax breaks and entitlements for the wealthy, we fall to the bottom of the class. Rattner says, "Our taxes are low by international standards, and our social welfare programs (to the poor) . . . are less generous."

We're basically good people, struggling to keep our economy moving forward. Yet the growth in wealth at the top isn't resulting in the growth of jobs, the lifeblood of our middle class. With good reason, those who are hoarding money simply don't trust the economy to give them a return — or simply allow them to break even. As a result, most of the population is losing faith in free-enterprise capitalism and in our government's ability to lead the country through this crisis.

Free enterprise doesn't offer the opportunity it once did for all our people. Lifting regulations has helped those at the top, leaving behind too many others. Unintentionally, we've stoked the greed of those who can take advantage of looser regulations and make incomparable wealth on Wall Street through arcane financial instruments, high-speed trading, and banking laws that mix consumer and investment banking. It's unsustainable. We keep riding bubbles that give us the illusion of growth until they burst, and then we wonder why, each time, we seem even worse off than eight or ten years earlier. We've forgotten the wisdom in the phrase "too good to be true."

Our house of cards became so shaky that only the actions of the Federal Reserve and a series of federally backed bailouts enabled us to avoid another Great Depression in 2008. These saved us, but the effects of that intervention haunt us now. The question remains whether we avoided a depression or merely postponed it. We've forgotten that this healthier-seeming economy is being propped up by near-zero interest rates that open floodgates of cheap cash from the Fed. Wall Street borrows and invests in stock buybacks to pump up stock prices and make a quick, winning gamble in the casino of the New York Stock Exchange. But those quick and dirty loans don't nourish Main Street. The choices made by the Fed have created only the *simulation* of actual growth that we're experiencing now. We face game-changing technologies that replace human beings and the flat earth of global competition. We need a new vision for government's role and a political system that adapts to these new forces.

Ken and I see clearly the emerging reality of choices that business must make. Do we respond and lead — in fact *demand* that we change our ways in business? Yes, government can play a critically important role in helping drive the economy, making it easier to do business; it can fix our unfair, unworkable, and outdated tax system and more. But as Ken and I reflected, reforming our broken-down, gridlocked political system is above and beyond the scope of what we business people can hope to accomplish in the short term. So who is best to fix the way business should operate in the future?

First, we in business are culpable in creating the inequality of income that resulted in the inequality of opportunity crisis. And now we must decide to be part of the solution. Sitting back, hoping that the government can agree to move with alacrity and purpose in this era of gridlock, would simply be irresponsible. We are running out of time, so we capitalists must arise. If we don't, as we will see in the next chapter, our culture and our current path will continue to take us down a scary rabbit hole.

BUSINESS HAS BECOME ITS OWN OPPONENT

As of now, the business sector offers our only prospect for leadership. The tribal animosity of Washington offers little hope for intelligent, swift response. Business can accept the challenge if its leaders can find the will to act now.

The private sector has to face its central role in our economic stagnation, with all the resulting social ills that have sprung up around it. Is free-market capitalism obsolete — is it destined to destroy itself, as Karl Marx predicted? Or has something else happened to twist capitalism into something it didn't need to be? We'll cut to the chase: it's the latter.

Free-market capitalism has been hijacked. Understanding how that happened is the next step. It's a saga about how a philosophy of short-term shareholder primacy became the guiding principle of both business management and Wall Street. In turn, this tragic misdirection of free-market capitalism joined forces with technology, globalization, the creation of a "protected" upper class (as Peggy Noonan has referred to it), and unwise and uncaring government actions, and together those forces have created the unstable, scary, and unsustainable socioeconomic system that has grown up around us over the past four decades.[9] In effect, shareholder primacy fuels a state of patrimony, where a favored minority uses its income to buy influence in order to perpetuate its control and power.

So, yes, we business leaders must be held partly responsible for the challenging crisis we, in fact, helped create. But, also importantly, business can help lead to wise solutions to these challenges, as we'll discuss in the coming pages.

5.

SHAREHOLDER VALUE GETS LEAN AND MEAN

IN MY TWENTIES, WHEN I was closer to the bottom than the top at Young & Rubicam, I had a front-row seat at a drama that revealed to me the heart of free-market capitalism in one of its finest moments. It became an episode much studied in the following years for the way a particular CEO acted with integrity, courage, and moral grit — and by doing so, he rescued his company's hopes for a profitable future. In the short term, he faced an enormous hit to the firm's market value and the possibility that his tenure at the helm would be viewed as a catastrophic failure. And yet he didn't flinch. Short-term shareholder value was the last thing on his mind.

The corporation was Johnson & Johnson. The year was 1982. On the morning of September 29, in Elk Grove Village, Illinois, an unsuspecting mother opened a bottle of Tylenol and gave her feverish twelve-year-old daughter, Mary Kellerman, a capsule that turned out to be tainted. Mary was dead by 7 p.m. — poisoned by potassium cyanide believed to have come from the Tylenol. In rapid succession, six more people in the Chicago region died after ingesting cyanide-laced Tylenol.

At the time, J&J's product was the best-selling pain reliever in the country, an enormous cash cow for the manufacturer. As it was later discovered, the bottles of Tylenol had been tampered with after they'd left the factory, so J&J wasn't at fault. But the most urgent question at that time was how to protect the public and identify the rest of the deadly analgesic.

It looked at first like a no-win nightmare for Jim Burke, the conglomerate's CEO. He could have done any number of things to deflect responsibility. He might have shifted the burden to retail outlets, asking them to take responsibility for what they sold, and thus saved his short-term profits. Or he could have recalled all bottles of the product from that region. Or he might have simply delayed and done nothing, gambling that all the other tainted bottles had been found. The most punishing alternative was to take full responsibility. None of these choices had a good outcome for the immediate bottom line.

Burke convened an urgent meeting of his direct reports. He called Ed Ney, Y&R's chairman and CEO, and Alex Knoll, our president, and asked them to fly in for the meeting. He wanted Y&R's full attention for the announcement he was about to make because we would have to make sure it was communicated effectively to the public. Burke already knew what a bombshell this would be. But he felt he had no choice.

I was a young account executive at the time, lucky enough to be good at taking notes. It was the evening of that first day by the time we arrived at J&J's headquarters in New Brunswick, New Jersey, yet we convened immediately. Burke was troubled by what he knew he had to do. After some initial casual conversation — he was a close friend with both of our leaders — he opened a drawer and pulled out a sheet of paper. It was a printout of the Johnson & Johnson credo, a famous document about corporate ethics. In front of top management and his small crew of envoys from Young & Rubicam, he simply read the document aloud. This is essentially what he said (with minor changes that J&J has since made to the credo):

> We believe our first responsibility is to the doctors, nurses and patients, to mothers and fathers and all others who use our products and services. In meeting their needs everything we do must be of high quality. We must constantly strive to reduce our costs in order to maintain reasonable prices. Customers' orders must be serviced promptly and accurately. Our suppliers and distributors must have an opportunity to make a fair profit.

We are responsible to our employees, the men and women who work with us throughout the world. Everyone must be considered as an individual. We must respect their dignity and recognize their merit. They must have a sense of security in their jobs. Compensation must be fair and adequate, and working conditions clean, orderly and safe. We must be mindful of ways to help our employees fulfill their family obligations. Employees must feel free to make suggestions and complaints. There must be equal opportunity for employment, development and advancement for those qualified. We must provide competent management, and their actions must be just and ethical.

We are responsible to the communities in which we live and work and to the world community as well. We must be good citizens — support good works and charities and pay our fair share of taxes. We must encourage civic improvements and better health and education. We must maintain in good order the property we are privileged to use, protecting the environment and natural resources.

Our final responsibility is to our stockholders. Business must make a sound profit. We must experiment with new ideas. Research must be carried on, innovative programs developed and mistakes paid for. New equipment must be purchased, new facilities provided and new products launched. Reserves must be created to provide for adverse times. *When we operate according to these principles, the stockholders should realize a fair return* [emphasis added].[1]

These were words written decades earlier by General Johnson, the corporation's founder, and they laid out exactly what it meant to be a successful, responsible corporation. The words were well known to everyone in the room. They were essentially corporate scripture. Shareholder value came last in time — one needed to be patient to see that return — but not least. All the other factors added up to shareholder value, given time to come together in the creative synergy of new products and new markets, generated by these fundamental principles. It was a moral vision, but more importantly, it was a practical one — it was what enabled a capitalistic enterprise to thrive in a way beneficial to everyone it touched.

In paragraph one, Burke recited his organization's *number one stakeholder*, its customers: the patients, doctors, and nurses who relied on J&J to deliver effective, safe products. Next came the employees. They needed to be treated fairly, compensated adequately, and offered benefits that would enable them to live with a sense of economic and physical security and have a hope for a better future. The third paragraph was about the communities in which J&J did business.

"This is where these horrible murders happened. These are the people we failed," I remember Burke saying. "We have to make sure this never happens again."

The final paragraph stated that if the company does all these things well, the shareholder — last but not least — will get a fair return on his or her money and will continue to invest in a company with a promising long-term future.

"We have twenty-four hours to figure out the right thing to do," Burke said. "I think I know what that is. But I want you all to tell me what you think."

In the end, everyone agreed with what he already knew he had to do. As a result, his company recalled every last bottle of Tylenol from the US market. It was the first mass recall of a product in the country's history. He very quickly followed with the introduction of a creative innovation that spread throughout the food and drug industry: the tamper-proof container.

The cost of all this was punishingly steep. The price of doing the right thing often is — in the short term. Almost half the company's market value dropped away. The next few weeks had to have been filled with dark, sleepless nights for Burke. He'd done nothing wrong, and yet it was as though one madman had come close to bringing down a corporate giant, a household name. But within a few months, J&J's stock value surpassed its precrisis value by a surprising percentage. The honesty and integrity of this company, which acted above and beyond what the public would have expected from a profit-making enterprise, actually paid off in a huge way. The decision to put short-term profits aside for the sake of the company's most important stakeholder — the customer — was not only the right thing to do, it was also good business management. If Jim Burke had been concerned only about short-term shareholder value, his company might not have survived that assault on its brand's integrity.

So many years later, sitting across the desk from Ken Langone, I recalled the details of this story. We wondered how our current business culture had strayed so far from the integrity Burke displayed — risking everything to protect the safety of his customers, doing the right thing even when he knew short-term profits might suffer a terrible blow.

"When I describe what's happening to our economy as a result of short-sighted greed, many business leaders tell me, 'The market will solve the problem. The market will take care of it,'" I told Ken.

"I get that, too. It won't. You and I both know that."

"It may have been true back when the free market was genuinely more free."

"We've gotten too big for it. Markets become easy to manipulate now," he said.

In a pre Industrial Age village, supply and demand might find a balance naturally, as would prices and pay. But to achieve the natural balance between supply and demand in the modern era, we need rules of engagement — explicit and unspoken — that ensure that owners enjoy a good profit while workers earn a living wage.

I'm not sure whether Adam Smith's "invisible hand" was ever completely free to do its work for the good of everyone in an economy. At some level, we've always had to *consciously* balance the interests of owners and workers, of sellers and buyers. There were always rules of conduct that helped regulate the market in a way that enabled the system to weather extremes: a dearth in supply, a loss of demand, or a surplus of labor. There are limits to what we can influence. Nothing could have saved the buggy whip from the arrival of the automobile, but when our economy was running well, we had both business leaders and Washington taking conscious steps to make sure workers, customers, and communities all thrived — even during disruptions. Why? One simple reason: it worked. It was the right way to keep making a profit.

The J&J credo considers self-evident that private enterprise can thrive only if it respects a symbiotic relationship between business and the surrounding social order. Business and society are tied together, inextricably, in a relationship that, like a good marriage, has to be sustained over time. It's a recognition also embedded in the original concept of a free market itself. A competitive market that allows the best and strongest businesses to thrive allows prices to freely adjust to supply and demand, but it isn't free in the sense that the private sector operates in a state of anarchy. Competition happens within a set of artificial rules of engagement — covenants, both legal and moral, including codes of behavior, such as the J&J credo, that simply articulate the factors essential for growth. (We all imagine the Ten Commandments as a moral code, but they are also a how-to manual on happiness and prosperity. They actually work as fatherly advice on how best to thrive in life.) These codes of behavior, as essential as they are, often remain implicit, but they are a reflection of the consensus of our society and business community. An obvious example: antitrust laws designed to pre-serve competition when it's possible to extinguish it by letting the most powerful players consolidate ownership or fix artificially high prices among all providers of a service or product. A slightly mod-ified version of the J&J credo really could serve as an articulation of a new stakeholder-primacy philosophy, in place of shareholder primacy. It honors the need to optimize multiple stakeholders for the health of the whole system, both the business and the com-munity at large. It is most importantly a *practical* document: fol-low it and you will win; stray from it, and you will eventually fail.

We've lost the ecological sense of balance embodied in that credo — a kind of systems thinking — that once acted as an internal barometer for our most successful captains of industry, and that still drives people like Bill Gates, Warren Buffett, Ken Langone, James Sinegal (of Costco), and many other quiet heroes who take the broadest perspective and the longest view of what free-market capitalism is really about.

SHAREHOLDER VALUE IS ERODING REAL VALUE

Today, the vast majority of businesses are run with only one sim-ple metric for success: to produce the highest possible profit each quarter. For now, these companies continue to get that job done.

The stock market, for now, is booming. As a result, the new managerial class — often compensated with shares of stock — effectively siphons wealth from the system without having to contribute commensurate new value to the economy. Matthew Yglesias of *Slate* and *Vox* writes:

> We're tasting the bitter fruit of the "shareholder value" revolution. Executives at publicly traded companies are paid to generate higher share prices, which is done by hitting quarterly earnings targets. This leads to underinvestment ...
> not because managers of private firms are indifferent to the [long-term] interests of shareholders, but because there's less need ... [to connect] compensation, share price, and quarterly earnings.[2]

All of this was justified nearly four decades ago by a philosophy popularized by Milton Friedman's famous piece in the *New York Times* extolling the practice of "shareholder value" as the only legitimate goal of business. In recent decades that idea has degraded into the pursuit of short-term gain.[3] The faster the profit, the better. Milton Friedman's rule was crucially narrowed to maximize *short-term* shareholder value. Thus, shareholder primacy began.

It's important to recognize that this is a relatively new phenomenon. As early as 1981, the Business Roundtable stated: "Corporations have a responsibility, first of all, to make available to the public quality goods and services at fair prices, thereby earning a profit that attracts investment, provides jobs, and builds the economy."[4]

This, of course, was totally consistent with a view of how the "market" was supposed to function. Johnson & Johnson's response to the Tylenol episode captured its essence. To quote again from the company's brilliant credo:

> We are responsible to our employees, men and women who work with us around the world. Everyone must be considered as an individual. We must respect their dignity and recognize their merit. They must have a sense of security in their work. Compensation must be fair and adequate. There must be equal opportunity for development and advancement for

the qualified. We must provide competent management and their actions must be just and ethical.

Once again, the credo concludes: "Our final responsibility is to stockholders. Business must make a sound profit. When we operate according to these principles, the stockholder should realize a fair return."

With a stroke of the pen, Milton Friedman disregarded both the letter and spirit of *this* free-market capitalism — the type that built America as the strongest economy on the planet. It had been an amazing period in America's history, a unique era of success. An age in which we came closest to the democratic vision of the Founding Fathers. It was a time when business recognized and understood that it was the source of social good in which a better life for all was the ideal that regulated how business pursued success. When Friedman shifted this focus toward protecting short-term profits instead of long-term gains, he inspired a countertrend, a disastrous shift that would culminate in the crisis we face today.

The shareholder primacy manifesto created by Friedman spawned the justification for the hijacking of free-market capitalism, which had, until then, driven the greatest economic surge in history. It was the inception of the long slide that has taken us to where we are today. A bevy of factors added fuel to this destructive fire:

- The deregulation of business practices favoring owners and corporations over labor.

- The loss of bargaining power among unions (sending unions into self-destruct mode by fighting the wrong battles).

- The increasing view that employees are simply the steepest cost of doing business—a cost to be reduced whenever possible.

- The flatlining of wages in America, even as productivity and profits grow unimpeded.

- The advent of leveraged buyouts that put pressure on management to prove itself every quarter so as to avoid loss of control.

- The way money now creates more money on Wall Street, without creating value in the actual market of goods and services.

Corporate profit margins are at an all-time high, even though the entire economy has nearly stalled, and wages have barely kept up with inflation for the past forty years. Not so with our profits. In a recent review of "Business in America," the *Economist* made a bold but powerful, and extremely unorthodox, claim: "Profits are too high."[5]

A case in point is the airline industry. Once upon a time, running an airline was a difficult financial proposition. Not anymore. In 2015, America's airlines made $24 billion — more than Google's parent company. That spectacular performance came with roughly flat revenues — thank the collapse of oil prices for this sudden windfall. Yet none of this sudden good fortune accrued to passengers or employees. Fares maintained altitude. Wages didn't take off. Service to passengers remained minimal or dropped from poor to revolting. (I flew from Florida to Phoenix recently and had the worst service I can recall anywhere in the world — and I feel as though I have logged as many flight miles in the course of my life as George Clooney's character in *Up in the Air*.)

What is true of the airline industry is true on a global basis with businesses big and small. Profits improve while everything else lags behind. Even as US businesses have seen the biggest increases in profit margins, the simple reality is that only the shareholders win, while consumers, employees, and the corporations themselves continue to lose (see figure 7).

In a seminal essay in *Harvard Business Review*, economist William Lazonick of the University of Massachusetts at Lowell echoes our account of the damage that shareholder primacy has done to our economy.[6] The title of his article tells the story: "Profits Without Prosperity." Corporations routinely devote 91 percent of their earnings to shareholders, not to research, development, new business initiatives, or adequate cost-of-living raises for ordinary employees.

All of that nonproductive effort is driven by a willful blindness to how destructive the pursuit of shareholder value has become.

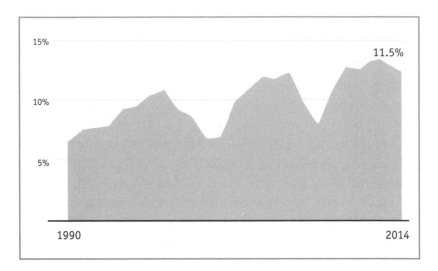

FIGURE 7: Corporate profit margins are at an all-time high

We have reached an insatiable appetite for more; a certain kind of success breeds more of itself. Most employee costs get cut while CEOs and top management's wealth reaches legendary levels. Even worse, the top twenty-five hedge fund managers, for example, made $25 billion in 2013. And in 2015, the CEOs of the largest investment and commercial banks had increases in compensation of $25 million more.

The chart in figure 8 is one of the most vivid demonstrations of the role business plays in contributing to income inequality. Productivity and profit margins, as figure 7 shows, have increased dramatically. Not wages. Real wages have stayed flat or have declined since mid-1970. (Note: In figure 8, hourly compensation is of production/nonsupervisory workers in the private sector, and productivity is for the total economy.)

In a recent issue, the *Economist* cited data showing that "The decline in the share of output going to workers over the past decade is equivalent to about 60 percent of the rise in domestic corporate pre-tax profits."[7]

Despite the extraordinary rise in income and wealth for the top income quartile in America, the median household income today is less than 1 percent higher than it was in 1989. And since the 2008

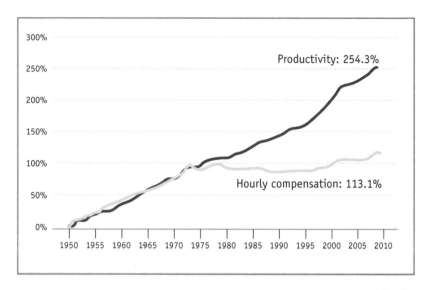

FIGURE 8: The growth of real hourly compensation for production/non-supervisory workers and productivity, 1948–2011.

financial crisis, 91 percent of income growth has gone to the top 1 percent. Flat wages have taken a serious bite out of far too many people's standard of living.

Yet the money is there. The *Economist* estimates that the excess cash generated in the United States by corporations, beyond their investment budgets, runs at a staggering $800 billion annually. Yes, billion. Per year. That represents 4 percent of the GDP. The money is certainly out there, often hidden in foreign subsidiaries. The losers are wages, above all, and then adequate levels of R&D, which would create more businesses and more jobs. Indeed, there is something tragically wrong with how our free-enterprise system is working now.

As the economy began to rebound from the 2008 crisis, we kept hearing that GDP was crawling up, that more jobs were being created, but wages have remained stubbornly flat. On top of that, as figure 9 shows, total spending on labor as a percentage of GDP has been decreasing — horrific news for both our economy and our society.

Where else are corporations stinting? After wages, R&D is the

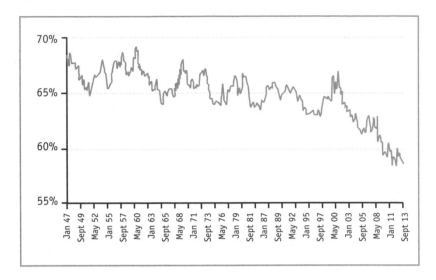

FIGURE 9: Total spending on labor as a percentage of GDP

second most-important factor for the long-term future of any company, as well as the American economy as a whole, and this indicator would suggest R&D is the other major loser in our current economic system. Figure 10 shows the chronic decrease in R&D as a percentage of GDP over the past three decades.

And the future development of new businesses and new ideas

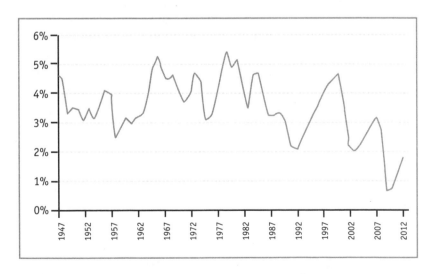

FIGURE 10: US business investment as a percentage of GDP

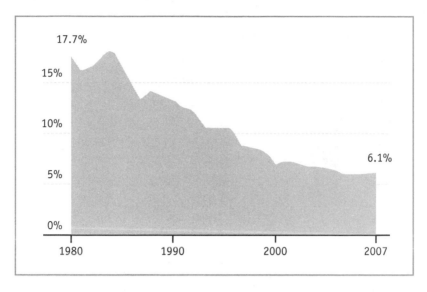

FIGURE 11: Share of US companies publishing new scientific research

looks totally depressing. As figure 11 shows, US companies lag behind other developed nations in publishing new scientific research — indicating a clear sign of our future lack of competitiveness.

And even more specifically, in dollars and cents, you can see in figure 12 the change in R&D expenditures in the United States vs. other nations, which is another disastrous trend.

Since 1980, managing a company to hike short-term shareholder

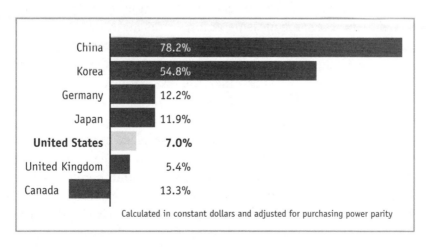

FIGURE 12: Change in business expenditures on R&D, 2009–13

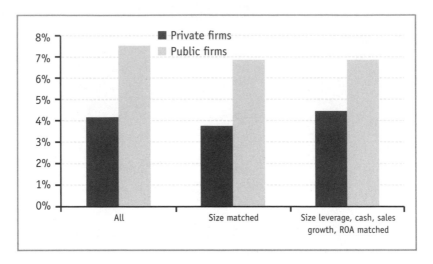

FIGURE 13: Investment rates for private firms vs. public firms (percent of total assets)

value caught on in public companies, but not private ones. Private owners want long-term profits; they want the companies they created to survive. Their CEOs grow them cautiously, and they keep the entire organization functioning at its most creative capacity, because they aren't going to move on to some other post in three years. So it's instructive to compare returns on assets at public and private firms, as figure 13 shows.

This chart shows three measures: total public (gray) vs. private investment; the same measure among firms matched by size; and again with firms matched by size, cash, sales, and growth. The ratio is essentially the same across the chart. Private companies perform better in all cases. R&D can increase productivity sometimes by eliminating jobs. That has traditionally been an appropriate way to justify R&D spending — and new digital technology is constantly being generated that has the potential to replace human workers. But R&D is also extraordinarily effective in creating new jobs, first by expanding the quality of current brands — and therefore growing markets — and by dramatically expanding corporate interests into line extensions or related businesses. Research is a vital spur to creativity and innovation, the drivers of new products and services.

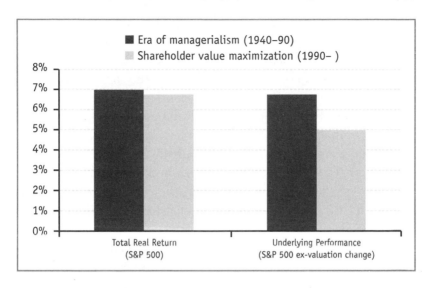

FIGURE 14: Returns by era

All of this provides a company with competitive differentiation, helps fulfill customer needs, and ultimately creates new markets and industries. Examples of this in today's world are impressive. New pharmaceuticals, new products that spur entirely new product categories — the smartphone, for example — and new ways to generate sustainable energy are three obvious examples of innovation that creates new jobs. The simple software programs that enable websites — and businesses — to spring up, that encourage people to rent their homes to visitors, have, along with Uber, generated a whole new category of trade: people who are now able to make money by lending property or offering simple skills to others in need of them.

Figure 14 also makes inescapably clear how the philosophy of shareholder-value maximization deprives the economy of real economic value. The period from 1945–80, and the more current decades, show almost identical total market returns. But the underlying performance of corporate assets is significantly lower. That's an example of how shareholder primacy destroys real value.

Our public corporations are no longer generating as much new value — in products and services — to grow profit. Instead, they are increasing profit by allowing their core assets to languish while they engineer higher share prices through financial manipulation. Through stock buybacks, companies are reducing the number of shares and thus increasing share value. At the same time, executives are increasing dividends to shareholders, shunting profit into the accounts of stockholders, including themselves, and neglecting both employees and R&D.

Public companies now will typically channel cash flow into a stock buyback rather than investment in plants and equipment, and thus new jobs. At the same time, they will cut costs, such as wages and R&D, to boost earnings per share. As William Gross has pointed out, "Never have American companies sent a greater share of their sales to the bottom line. Even when S&P 500 companies have witnessed a decline in corporate earnings, they still have experienced earnings-per-share gains."[8]

Part of the justification for this philosophy is that shareholders are viewed as the equivalent of owners in a private company. The prevailing myth is that shareholders own the corporation. As Lynn Stout, a Cornell Law School professor, has pointed out conclusively, this isn't legally the case.[9] She writes that shareholders don't legally own a company: they simply own shares of stock. The corporation itself owns its assets. The shareholders have rights, but so do other stakeholders. If they were true owners, shareholders would be liable in a court of law for a corporation's mistakes and crimes. They aren't. Shareholders are more like renters than owners.

Executive compensation strategies, along with our tax code, only reinforce this passion for shareholder value. So much compensation now is tied to stock price: an executive's compensation in large part comes from shares of stock in the company that he or she runs. If an executive wants to earn more, she or he has to boost the company's stock price by any means, regardless of what it does to the company's ability to generate long-term value or provide employees with adequate compensation. Shareholder pressure aligns perfectly with a CEO's own five-year career plans. It's an unholy alliance.

To incentivize shareholder primacy, CEOs get paid extraordinary amounts. During our Golden Age, a CEO typically was paid twenty times the average of what his employees were making.

Today, that ratio is anywhere from 400 to 600 times the employees' wage. And the CEO has little time to establish any kind of long-term vision or strategy because the usual tenure for the top dog is now less than four years.

Not surprisingly, CEO tenure matters. A recent analysis by S&P Global Market Intelligence, done for *USA Today,* showed that the companies run by the most-tenured CEOs exceed the performance of all others by about 25 percent.[10]

Shareholder activists have become one of the key drivers of short-term shareholder maximization. Their practice used to be to work through management to offer ideas and suggestions to improve a corporation's return for the long term. Even when shareholder activists totally lost confidence in a company's management and board and took over the company, they did so with a noble purpose. They did it because they believed they could build greater value for the company and wanted to see that greater return over time. Alas, those constructive activists are still around, but in smaller numbers. The new activists are hedge fund–type owners who have the shortest possible view of increasing returns. They are more like terrorists who manage through fear and strip the company of its crucial underlying assets, and then sell it back to the market with grossly diminished chances of long-term success.

At this point, they resemble hostage-taking terrorists — with the CEO as the prize hostage. Warren Buffet has said that his favorite holding period for a stock is forever. Not for this group. This greedy gang strips a company down to the leanest, meanest core, extracting cash out of everything that would otherwise generate long-term value — like a runner burning muscle in the last miles of a marathon — and then abandons the company entirely, moving on to do the same somewhere else.

CEOS HAVE BEEN TAKEN HOSTAGE

I want to give you a sense of the power that a shareholder activist can wield without ever lifting a finger or saying a word. Even when they don't do a thing, they exert an oppressive, controlling influence on the management of our largest corporations.

For more than a year, starting in April 2015, I've been having a long-distance debate with the CEO of one of the fifty largest Fortune 500 corporations. I'll call him Jerry Bauer here to respect his privacy. He was completely open and honest with me about the pressures he faces as a CEO. He knew I faced them as well when I took Y&R public before I retired. Yet what he told me in confidence might be seen as a liability by shareholder activists who think it's their job to keep people in Jerry's position on their toes — by that I mean in fear of losing their jobs, and the fear of losing the company through a hostile takeover.

His company's brand is familiar to everyone, and Jerry's actual name is extremely well known among the business community. He's a heavyweight who has done remarkable things for his famous company. And, as you might guess, he's a busy guy, so I'm flattered that he has taken the time to give serious thought to the issues in this book.

He agrees that the private sector's priorities need to change, and he is blunt about whether he himself will be able to change the way he runs his own company. My dialog with him illuminates what Ken Langone and I have been facing, along with others who are calling for change, when it comes to changing key principles of business management in an environment of economic stress. Let's be honest. We're asking for CEOs to put aside one or two core imperatives that have governed the key measure of whether they are rated as effective leaders. Let's just say that acting on such a proposal is not the sort of thing that falls within a business executive's comfort zone.

Jerry and I met at his headquarters in the fall of 2015. I took him through a slide show of the charts in this book, weaving into the data my argument that free-market capitalism has reached a dead end. At first he was dubious about the notion that our system was in deep trouble, yet he paid close attention to the numbers and was stunned at some of the charts. We talked at some length without really disagreeing about the economic impasse we've reached in the United States.

"Everyone knows we're in a bad spot right now," Jerry said. "Look at the presidential campaigns. But your numbers really do clarify how bad it is."

"The upshot of all of it is that right now we need higher wages across the board," I said. "It's the only way to get enough money circulating through the system again."

He smiled, probably at the thought of trying to convince his board of directors to do such a thing.

"Well, you may be right, Peter. In fact, I think you probably *are* right. But — " Jerry said, still smiling. He knew he didn't have to finish that sentence.

"I know," I said. "But I could help you make a case for it."

"I can't do this alone. I mean, I can't be the only CEO who steps up and announces higher wages, out of the blue."

"Walmart did."

"Not at the scale you're talking about. I'd get crucified at the next shareholder meeting. I think you're right. But it's suicide for somebody in my position."

"I agree we need a whole cohort of business leaders to stand up and commit to higher wages. But that would be easier if a few brave souls got it started."

"I'm not one of them right now."

"Let me help you make a case for it," I said.

"Knock yourself out. If I think I can take what you send me to the board and get agreement, maybe we can do it. I can't make any promises."

So in the ensuing months, I've continued the conversation by sending him supportive documents and data, hoping to break through his reservations. The interesting aspect of this struggle is that he agreed with my stance: the economy is structurally in trouble, and the private sector needs to act now to turn it around, simply to ensure the continuation of our economic system. But . . . he would be a target for shareholder activists who would work to unseat him as quickly as possible. He would need cover.

The problem is the shadow of the guillotine that lingers at the back of Jerry's mind, and in the boardroom where the activists would assemble to take him apart, if he ever acted on the urgency of what needs to be done by raising compensation across the board and fine-tuning his company for long-term growth rather than short-term profit.

WHAT CAN YOU DO ABOUT IT?

At this point, it may well be worth remembering Peter Drucker's simple admonition: "The only valid purpose of a firm is to create a customer."[11] In our current era, we've forgotten how to create nearly everything other than a spurious profit, which will become harder and harder to achieve with each passing year.

The mystery of why free-market capitalism, as we're now practicing it, cannot rectify our inequality of opportunity is pretty clear. The free-market capitalism that built America into an economic, social, and military powerhouse is no more. It's a shadow of its former self. Shareholder value has been debased into a machine that rewards one stakeholder — the person who owns shares — at the tragic expense of all the rest: the employees, the customers, the communities, and the nation itself. This practice, now deeply embedded in our public markets and our business culture around the world, is both destructive and unsustainable, as our system eats itself away.

Yet convincing CEOs to change (one by one) is hard. Very hard. After a dozen or more meetings, Ken and I found just how hard it will be to turn this ship. It's not that any single CEO disagreed that the problem is severe, urgent, and consequential. The answer we get is simply: "What can I do about it?"

I believe the more relevant question today is a new one: What *must* a CEO do?

The devastating consequence of rising income inequality, which drives the inequality of opportunity in a majority of American communities, is sounding a deafening alarm. We've already demonstrated an urgent need for societal and economic change. It's up to business now to do what it can and what it must to contribute to solutions. Why? Because it will work — for *everyone*, including the shareholder.

6.

THE WAY FORWARD

IN THE MID-1990S, alone in my office, I was preparing for a major meeting with AT&T's still newish CEO and top management. For some time, AT&T had been struggling. Separate from operational issues, a number of business initiatives that had been a slam dunk in the past just weren't working. I got the call to meet with AT&T's top team and explain our view of what was happening in the marketplace. It wasn't a strange request. I'd had the same concern for some time, and several other clients were struggling with similar issues. What we needed weren't just new tactics or new communication efforts. First we needed to grasp the fundamental changes in the marketplace — changes that created an unfamiliar discomfort, a sense of dislocation. The old tactics weren't effective. We were at a loss.

The epiphany came with a song that popped into my head. R.E.M. had released "It's the End of the World as We Know It," and it concluded with the words "I feel fine." The world felt as though it were ending, yet we felt anything but fine. Those lyrics were like a taunt. I needed to know just what it took to feel fine in a new and unrecognizable world. In the days to follow, with that song playing in my head, I figured out the new rules of engagement.

The business world as we knew it was coming to an end. It would take another decade for the new reality to fully set in. In fact, it turned out there were not one, but two seismic shifts underway, and I understood only one of them before the AT&T meeting. I wouldn't catch up with the second until after the 2008 collapse.

Toward the end of the twentieth century, across the developed and the advanced developing nations, a quiet revolution took place under our noses. What occurred was a dramatic change in commerce from a world characterized by excess consumer demand to a world of excess supply of products and services. Scarcity no longer determined value. The forces of technology started this shift, and it continued rapidly into the twenty-first century. Industry by industry, excess supply became a law of commerce — even when those who were adapting to it didn't consciously recognize what was essentially a new law of economics.

With remarkably few exceptions, in every industry, multiple sources of supply can spring up and serve customers with the same quality of product or service. As a result, there is the potential for a surplus of nearly anything anyone needs or wants. We've reached a state of permanent excess supply. As a result, prices continuously fall. (One caveat: this can occur only if nations or societies have the will to allow the transition to happen. Oil faces artificial bottlenecks for various reasons, and diamonds are hoarded to reduce supply. And who knows why my cable broadband speeds are so much lower than they are in Europe. I suspect it isn't because the profit margin is too slim. But these are largely elective constraints.)

What has become clear is that in the world of excess supply, you need to do business in a dramatically different way from how it was done in the past. The balance of power has shifted from the manufacturer/provider to the customer. Customers, not CEOs, rule the world of business now. Multiple technologies, easy access to abundant capital, availability of low-cost manufacturing, and other factors quickly obscure or erase the qualities that differentiate competitive products. Everything slides to the rank of a commodity quickly and inevitably.

Consumers face a bewildering range of choices with almost no intrinsic variations. Too often, the only real difference is price. Any Google search for a hotel room through one of half a dozen websites that offer price comparisons illustrates this. Each website lists a dozen choices of rooms sorted by cost. The only constant is a relentless pressure on the supply of nearly anything to bring down its price in competition with other suppliers. Price becomes one of two key differentiators; the other is the stack of customer reviews that usually accompany the listings in these portals. (Another huge shift of power to the consumer.) As a result, the lowest price — for comparable quality — usually wins. This incessant price war inevitably forces companies to continue cutting costs to lower margins so that they can keep profits up. And this level of competition will only intensify.

So what's the real upshot of all this? There are truly only two ways out of this whirlpool of steadily falling prices. First, innovation. It differentiates a company and draws all eyes to whatever is new, at least until competitors can mimic it. So sustained innovation capacity is the real answer. It requires large investments in research and development, product improvements, and intelligent brand building — all of them inadequately funded today.

Creativity has become the most essential and fundamental source of success in the twenty-first century. It has replaced the power of capital itself. Once again, a fundamental new law of economics is operating. With the industrial revolution, capital was the mother of all wealth. It enabled manufacturing, distribution, marketing, and more. (It wasn't called *capitalism* for nothing.) Capital has become just another important resource, now relatively inexpensive and in excess supply. Just ask the Federal Reserve. Creative power, or innovation, has become the superior driver of added value and wealth.

What this actually means is that success depends on your workforce itself — a cadre of people individually thinking creatively on behalf of the customer. That may sound like a leap, but it isn't. Consumers rule a world of excess supply. Innovation, as well as personalized service, holds their attention. So consumer-oriented innovations and improvements — a personalization of the buying experience — have to be delivered at every point of contact between the brand and consumers, and your workers are the ones hovering around those points of contact.

The second critical principle that can pave the way to a revitalized capitalist system rests on a recognition of basic human values. They are becoming the core of a successful business strategy. Our obsessive commitment to the maximization of short-term shareholder rewards ignores these values: it's corrosive and destructive in the long run. It undermines long-term growth and ultimately undercuts profitability. Many companies are beginning to recognize that their workforce, the common employee, is the source of their success, not simply another cost on the balance sheet. In many ways, top management has relegated human values to the personal realm — family, church, and memberships — while ignoring them in the workplace. The drive to increase short-term shareholder value has given us all permission to live this sort of bifurcated life: brutal with workers, kind and generous with those outside the realm of work. It no longer works.

Sustained innovation and creativity depend on a work environment in which employees are recognized and rewarded properly for their crucial contributions. When fear and resentment drive productivity, creativity shuts down; studies have shown that the creative mind can thrive only in a peaceful, nurturing, supportive environment. In a world of excess supply, that creativity is the only basis for agile, adaptive growth.

Management doesn't need to lower the bar for achievement. It can be just as demanding as ever, but with a vision based on hope and compassion for workers — not threats and bullying, not exploitation, not the type of mindset that looks for any way to get the most from human beings while rewarding them as little as possible. This isn't a moralistic vision but a practical one. It recognizes the psychological realities of human motivation and creativity.

I recall some years ago receiving a brilliant book that I never got to read: *The Customer Comes Second*. (There's now a newer one, with the same message: *Employees First, Customers Second*.) I almost threw it away. Turning one page, I read, "Employees must come first." It was all I took away from the book — but it was everything we need to know right now. Satisfied employees are increasingly a corporation's vital source of profit because they control those crucial points of contact with customers — in fact, every employee, in any firm, is hardly more than two or three degrees of separation from the customer. It used to be said that what's good for General Motors is what's good for America. Now, what pleases and delights its customers is what's good for General Motors. And to achieve that delight, GM needs superior employees at all levels.

Excess supply isn't related to supply-side economics from the 1980s. That theory claimed that simply by increasing the physical supply of products and services, GDP would increase. That might work in a world of excess demand, with a thriving middle class. Increasing supply would satisfy built-up demands, so consumption and GDP would increase.

But those days are gone. In the excess-supply world, simply increasing production of existing products will inevitably have the effect of lowering prices and thus profits. Today and in tomorrow's world, supply-side economics cannot work — you'll simply end up with excess inventory.

Business has the most to gain from a healthy America, and the most to lose by social unrest or punitive taxation. Business can start the process in two steps:

- Invest in the actual value creators—the employees. Start compensating fairly, by which I mean a wage that enables employees to share amply in productivity increases and creative innovations. The fact that real wages have been flat for about four decades, while productivity has increased by 80 percent, shows this has not been happening. Before the early 1970s, wages and productivity were both rising. Now, most gains from productivity go to shareholders, not to employees.

- Businesses must invest aggressively in their own operations, directing profit into productivity and innovation to boost real business performance. Today, too many corporations reduce investment in research and development and spend more on superficial brand building. As a result, we see a general decline in the value of their brands and other assets. This trend also retards new business, hampers the growth of existing operations, and therefore reduces opportunities for job creation. To make up for those declines and for anemic revenues, businesses buy back their stock (now at record levels) and thus artificially boost earnings per share.

Here's what's beautiful about these two fundamental principles. They are the path toward success in a world of incessant downward pressure on price that transforms all products and services into commodities. And they are also the principles that will help the economy as a whole pull out of its current path toward collapse. If the entire private sector adopted these principles, it would not only see astonishing results in long-term profitability, it would also watch as its communities began to rebuild, education improved, and industry started to thrive once again on our own soil. We would have found a way to reverse many or all of the trends of the past forty years that have brought us to where we are now. We would have cracked the code of how to adapt and thrive in the global economy — as a fully functioning economy and community, not simply as a tiny percentile of shareholders.

All of this was confirmed for me not long ago at the Aspen Ideas Festival when I heard Zeynep Ton describe an almost identical vision of how success rests on the shoulders of employees. Her talk was based on her book *The Good Jobs Strategy: How the Smartest Companies Invest in Employees to Lower Costs and Boost Profits.*[1] This brilliant young professor from MIT's Sloan School of Management was preaching what I consider the new gospel for our private sector: recognize and reward the supreme importance of employees. In the process of doing exhaustive research into how American companies were finding wholesale access to products for resale to customers in the United States, she discovered something disheartening. She told *The Atlantic*: "You could get a product all the way from China to the store, and then the product would get stuck in the back and never make it to the floor. For a supply-chain person like me, this was heartbreaking."[2]

What had enabled a company to find the best supplier — by seeking the lowest-cost alternative — ended up foiling the entire strategy. Unmotivated, uncaring employees were sabotaging the company's success because they had been treated as if they were the same as the supply chain — a cost. Their morale was at rock bottom.

Ton saw the havoc this caused and realized that a company's fortune now pivots around the enthusiastic creativity of its employees. By recognizing employees for making crucial decisions and encouraging them to be the concierge for a customer's satisfaction and to embrace responsibilities that impact the bottom line, you can create a culture that justifies and necessitates higher pay. But higher wages alone won't cut it. Employees must feel that they are creating value for customers and the company every hour of the day — they must know they are earning higher wages for a reason.

Ton's timing couldn't be better. With more effective and empowered employees, there's an easy way to justify higher wages — and we need them now more desperately than ever before. If companies begin to follow Ton's advice, more money will flow into the emptiest pockets, and from there into the economy, as spending gains more and more momentum.

All this requires a long-term vision, requiring patience and wisdom and foresight, and it's long overdue — a corrective to the maximization of short-term shareholder value that has justified the way we do business for way too long.

***

We've reached an inflection point that makes human beings the most important single factor in business success. Qualified people are essential. The service industry needs well-seasoned professionals — plumbers, carpenters, electricians, and more. In manufacturing, it's the same story. We need people who can partner with the machines that are displacing their less-skilled counterparts — just as my surgeon partnered with his robot to remove my prostate.

In the book *Race Against the Machine*, authors Erik Brynjolfsson and Andrew McAfee make an interesting point. They say it has become a myth that computers are now better than human players. In reality, the consistent winners are actually human beings consulting with computers. People are still orchestrating the win, with help from digital technology. The way forward, they suggest, will arise when people find similar ways, in all fields, to innovate through human effort, assisted and augmented by technology. New industries can be spawned to replace and enhance the old.

I am involved in a hyperlocal digital-news venture, which is designed to fill the void left behind as the printed local-newspaper model is dying in market after market. The digital world can be leveraged, though not too easily, to produce a new, easy-to-use Internet product. Our venture or someone else's venture will inevitably make it happen. So it is that technology, the job destroyer, can be turned into a friend — albeit with the recognition that the jobs created may not be as plentiful as the ones being eliminated.

A NEW PARADIGM: BUSINESS IN THE LEAD

We know change is hard. Any change makes most of us dread new ideas because we become vested in what we've already achieved. We believe that the way things are is the way they must be. That's human reality. From many CEOs, I hear a response that goes like this: someone must break the ice; someone must lead; I don't want to be taking this risk alone. Well, many are doing that right now, and their results are all the proof anyone needs that the stakeholder model works. Companies such as Home Depot, Costco Wholesale, Whole Foods, Publix, Qualcomm, Starbucks, and Gravity Payments are taking steps and compensating employees more. These are the courageous green shoots we need. They need to become the example for others, which will turn these practices into a trend and then a movement.

As Ken and I talk to business leaders and try to drum up support for our cause, we find almost unanimous agreement on the nature of the problem and the urgent need for solutions. That's the good news. Our concern is action. We've been told by chief executives that to pay employees more fairly, they need more support from their boards, from prominent business leaders, from the media, and even from the government to combat the intense market pressure to maximize short-term shareholder returns.

Many continue to think the federal government should take steps to address inequality of opportunity through stimulus, actions by the Fed, and so on. (Many state and local governments are going broke.) It's true that despite the current political gridlock, government can act effectively on this issue on a bipartisan basis. In fact, over time, government can do a great deal more. For example, our overall tax code needs a complete reimagining. On an individual basis, the progressive tax structure should be continued. Whether taxes go up or not should not be written in stone. Government's role is to optimize the benefit of society at large, and there are times when the job of the government will demand tax increases. But in general, tax policy should be a function of balanced budgets and extraordinary efficiency in carrying out government's mission. What should its mission be? In the short term, take steps to create an environment for job growth. It must support business principles that encourage investment in corporations, keep businesses in the United States, and dramatically reduce regulations over all businesses to allow them to operate with greater ease and freedom. At the same time, regulations are essential, for example, to preserve fair and open competition, which enhance economic growth and prevent abuses of monopolistic power. Government and business partnerships, as we'll discuss later, will be of critical importance to the well-being of the country.

But who can wait for that to happen? What about other stakeholders?

Philanthropy represents an extraordinary contribution to our society, to our culture, to our education, to our healthcare, to supporting many in need. It is a culture unique in the world, and it makes an immense impact on everyone's well-being. But philanthropy doesn't have the leverage nor the scope to address the systemic problems, which essentially come down to how our currently profitable private enterprise can recycle its healthy profits beyond the confines of Wall Street. Business presides over the balance sheet, the budget, and the payroll. The choice about whether to invest in workers rests on the shoulders of those who have, in recent years, considered the workforce as little more than the biggest cost of doing business. To continue viewing employees this way is a recipe for either economic collapse — the dramatic loss of demand for products that would follow mass insolvency — or social unrest.

Business needs to take action that's both simple and obvious, and such action would have an immediate impact on consumer confidence, retail sales, and economic growth in general. If businesses across the board began to invest more in their workforce, the effects would be dramatic and profound — not only in terms of the economy as a whole, but for its impact on the health of the business itself. Many companies are doing this now, and have been doing it for years: their phenomenal success is testimony to the power of these simple human values.

In a recent white paper, William Galston of the Brookings Institution imagined a way forward that proposed that government make full employment its top priority and suggested that business should focus on raising wages, especially in an era when profits are at record highs and cash is plentiful.[3]

TOWARD A FREE-MARKET CAPITALISM THAT ACTUALLY WORKS

The objectives are simple and clear: to compensate and treat employees appropriately and to invest more aggressively in R&D. The goals: sustained innovation and the growth it generates. The challenge is to get down to a more granular level: specific actions a CEO might take. What follows are possibilities. No single suggestion can fit every organization's unique character, its stage of life, and its competitive environment. Still, the majority of these suggestions can be implemented to some degree in most companies.

Most importantly, business, not government, must set the agenda for how companies should compensate their workers. Each company needs to adapt and adjust to the new normal with its own wisdom and flexibility, given the dynamics within that company and its industry. In addition, consideration should be given to the most efficient and effective way to improve compensation for employees outside the C-suite.

The first imperative is to increase compensation for employees making $100,000 or less. The source of these funds would come from a reasonable, incremental sharing of productivity and innovation gains — in other words, when leadership finds new ways to increase profit through efficiency, share it with employees as well as stockholders. (A decrease in the cost of financial engineering by throttling stock buybacks and lowering dividends could be shared this way as well). Depending on circumstances, the increase in compensation can be made in cash or equity — a form of restricted stock, for example. It could be a five-year plan that has a sunset and is reevaluated before continuing with appropriate improvements.

There are two fundamental concepts for how we can do this in a fair and just way. The first is a *fair wage*: that means sharing the incremental value produced by the organization as a result of productivity or innovation. That is fair value. The second way to do this is through a *living wage*. This applies to the lower end of the pay scale. Individuals should take home enough in wages to pay their bills, pure and simple. A living wage shouldn't be a single number across the board; it can differ depending on cost of living situations, based on different locations. Manhattan and Peoria will have different wage scales to achieve a living wage. So would Mumbai and Paris. We should think in those terms for everyone.

The plan would begin with meaningful yet modest raises, which would increase in size as the plan reaches its "new normal" for the percentage that's shared from gains from incremental revenues and profits. The new normal should be decided on the basis of long-term economic growth, not simply short-term profit. Over a period of time, the increases in the fair-wage concept should go all the way up to the C-suite. Rewards for real productivity and innovation should be awarded to all employees. The plan should be communicated broadly both inside the organization and publicly to the market and the general public. Companies that take steps like this find a media eager and willing to celebrate whatever helps the American worker and the middle class.

Meanwhile, the culture needs to shift toward a focus on long-term growth in real value. This means changing the mindset of management and the organizational culture. One such first step would be to ask the CEO's direct reports for their two best ideas for how to dramatically strengthen the corporation's long-term growth prospects and competitiveness. Select two or more of the projects for beta testing or outright implementation. Measure the progress of the projects and report broadly the projects' status against pre-set value-added metrics.

With this longer-term operating vision, develop rigorous multiyear operating plans. Demand from the organization ambitious goals for both existing businesses and innovative new products/businesses. Communicate to the market the vision, critical strategies, and targeted milestones along the way. Then, share equitably the incremental outcomes with leadership, all employees, the corporation's R&D needs, and shareholders.

Gradually manage to raise shareholder value while increasing investments in all employee compensation and corporate/product investment needs. This will redefine the parameters of how to measure long-term shareholder value and make growth more sustainable.

Behind all this has to be a strategy of building underlying assets:

- Measure annually the underlying value of the active, leverageable corporate assets. For example, annually monitor the value of the corporate brand and, most importantly, the value of a corporation's product or service brands. (Tools for measuring brand equity are available, which I'll mention later.)

- Develop specific action plans to leverage those brands and recognize and reward innovations and the value creators.

At the lower end of the pay scale, consider a living wage as the driving criteria. Recognize that the concept of a living wage should be developed with consideration for local and regional wage standards, as well as cost of living. A living wage must be realistic but also be perceived as generous in the context of its local and regional setting. Let me put it another way: pay people enough that it makes them feel lucky and privileged to work for you.

Though it isn't possible to offer remedial education to applicants who simply aren't qualified, a company should make continuing education a core element of its benefits program for all employees:

- Train employees and prospective employees for anticipated skill-level needs and develop partnerships with various educational institutions to help execute such plans. In Spartanburg, South Carolina, BMW has been running a special trade-school program. They take local high school graduates and put them through two years of training to become apprentice mechanics. It's a partnership with the local community and this enlightened car manufacturer. When they graduate, these young men and women are in most cases guaranteed full-time jobs at a pay rate above the national average.

- When terminating employees, provide for appropriate training or retraining of new or existing skills demanded by the marketplace.
- Embrace the concept of continuing education to increase value creation at all levels in the organization.

Finally, restructure executive compensation. Offer vesting of stock allocation over time. Peg salaries and bonuses on measures of long-term viability, not only on quarterly earnings growth. Examples of such goals include the following:

- Sustained profitability growth
- Focus on margins
- A new, more natural balance of employee compensation, R&D investment, and shareholder return
- Improvements/growth of underlying assets (brands)
- Other critical elements of the annual plan specific to industry and the company's competitive needs
- Tie CEO compensation to long-term objectives, not short-term gains
- Percentage increases for top management cannot be larger than the percentage increases for all other employees

LONGER-TERM GOVERNMENT AND PRIVATE INDUSTRY PARTNERSHIPS

The partnership between private and public realms has deep roots in American history. It's a crucial alliance for job creation. In healthcare, the Human Genome Project has produced an extraordinary wave of new jobs at several levels of the economy, many of them extremely well-paying jobs. Government's contribution has funded the basic research needed to sequence the genome. It would have been a task too large and too risky for private industry to undertake. Yet as soon as the basic research delivered the breakthroughs, private industry stepped in to monetize applications of the new knowledge. It worked beautifully, and it's still providing rewards through enhanced care and by creating meaningful, well-paying jobs.

The digital world provides another perfect example of public-private partnership: the Internet. First the government developed ARPANET, which then evolved into our Internet when private entrepreneurs flocked to the nascent network and built it into the infrastructure of our current virtual world. Companies that thrived and capitalized on the basic research involved in the Internet and World Wide Web are some of our current giants — Apple, Facebook, Google, Amazon, and Microsoft — as well as literally thousands of smaller companies and ventures. In fact, nearly any business that operates in America has a website and at least communicates via the Internet.

The possibilities of fundamental new knowledge and technology are staggering. Leaders created new industries by putting a man on the moon. Technology today can be harnessed to help create more profitable human jobs. It can be done, if only we have the will to make it happen.

In the short to medium term, government and private sectors can collaborate in many productive ways.

CREATE JOBS

First, let's start with the well-discussed critical need for rebuilding our crumbling infrastructure in cities and throughout the rest of the country: roads, railroads, airports, bridges, the electrical grid, subways, water pipes, and more.

Here's a way to get started. The idea came in a conversation I had with my good friend Michael, a brilliant businessman. He pointed out that companies have squirreled away close to three trillion dollars overseas, beyond the reach of US tax authorities. Repatriating those funds to the States would make it possible for businesses to direct that money into their own companies and create jobs in the process. As an incentive to have businesses bring back the funds, Congress could set a low tax rate for this purpose, for a limited period of time, of, say, 10 percent (although it could be higher). This idea has been proposed before, in the early 2000s, with some modest success. But here was Michael's big idea. Those tax dollars would be used exclusively for infrastructure projects.

More specifically, the funds would be deposited in a new bank with only one mission: invest in public- or private-sector projects judged as worthy investments in fixing various infrastructure needs. For example, if the total repatriation were to be $2.5 trillion, the tax revenue at 10 percent would be $250 billion. Leveraged at a ratio of 7:1, that amount could produce an asset base of $1.65 trillion. These are surely ballpark estimates, but in the range of common sense. That in turn could put millions of people to work on productive projects that would have many-fold benefits in providing jobs, improving the standard of living, providing significant economic growth, and making America more secure and economically more competitive.

Second, we can create a top technology task force, made up of the most successful tech companies. Their mission will be to develop technologies with a special intent to create jobs for human beings — more or less the opposite of what they've been doing: eliminating human labor. The role of the government in this process would be to invest in basic research. The decision to place a man on the moon, for example, generated large industries spun-off from research and inventions developed in that effort. The invention of the Internet, originally created by the government, has been an incalculable stimulus on economic growth. Innovations such as these from the government will have an impact soon on most spaces that human beings inhabit, through smart appliances and devices that will lead us into the age referred to as the Internet of Things. As for the future, let's think about investment in 3-D printing, nanotechnology, and sustainable energy sources.

EDUCATION

We can again serve as a model for the rest of the world, as we once did. The goal must become a national imperative: to build more effective secondary and higher education systems and to embark on a twenty-year initiative to provide early education for all children. We need to create a new trade-school system as an alternative to college. In Germany, some youngsters are recognized as more suited to trade schools than four-year colleges. We need a system of educational triage that directs students into the appropriate channels, based on aptitude and interest rather than the socioeconomic status of the parents.

❖❖❖

A brighter future calls for business to lead. In our society today, an enlightened business community constitutes the core competence of our culture for dealing with the complex challenges of our time. The practical vision and skill sets to solve social problems will come from the business world; so will the executional competence. But business must also rise to the challenge. It must realize that shareholder primacy is destructive and must evolve. Business needs to accept responsibility for the common good in our country. Yes, common sense and the common good must complement our current surplus of self-centered, me-first entitlement. The bounty that follows from the profit motive must be shared more fairly among a corporation's stakeholders. Can such an approach really work? The next chapter will prove that it has, it does, and it will.

STAKEHOLDER VALUE IS ALREADY WORKING

WE'VE TOLD THE STORY of the transformation in American business from a devotion to multiple stakeholders — when business had a much larger sense of its responsibility to its workers and the nation as a whole — to shareholder primacy. The magic of free-market capitalism that drove America from World War II up to the late 1970s was known for an allegiance to employees, customers, communities, the nation, and the economy itself. Now it has become a game of shareholder take all.

Yet there is much to celebrate in the way that many businesses are waking up to what a dead end this transformation has turned out to be. Hundreds of companies are practicing a smarter version of free-market capitalism every day — because they realize it's the only way to survive in the long run. The plea for business to abandon shareholder primacy may sound like an appeal to moral responsibility, but in reality it's a warning that only by giving up shareholder primacy will companies be able to keep rewarding shareholders. Some of these bellwether companies are very successful private firms; others are courageous and principled corporate leaders who have always known that the stakeholder model would yield better results, as well as being the right thing to do for individual workers and for the nation. By celebrating what these individual leaders and their companies are achieving, it's possible to imagine a tipping point, when the stakeholder model returns as the primary way we imagine a company's purpose.

Jim Sinegal is the son of a coal miner and steelworker. He grew up with a firsthand view of the realities of human labor and the difficulties of making a living through decades of sustained hard work, in his father's life and then in his own. What has endeared him to me the most may be that he's also a CEO who, at one point, has told unhappy shareholder activists to take a flying leap. He's the founder of Costco, one of the most successful retailers in the world, in an industry that's as tough as it gets. Few companies anywhere operate in an industry with lower margins. Costco is a public company, so it has no choice but to deliver top performance for shareholders. And yet, Sinegal founded the company with four simple, key principles:

1. Obey the law.
2. Treat customers fairly.
3. Treat employees fairly.
4. Respect suppliers.

You don't need an MBA to understand those basics. They equalize a CEO's devotion to the entire spectrum of stakeholders — not simply shareholders. If the company devotes itself to its employees, its customers, its suppliers, and the laws of its community, a profit will follow. Shareholders aren't even on the list, and yet they are a happy bunch. He has always adhered to those four cardinal rules, and he's been able to do it because he executed his strategy with superhuman organizational efficiencies. As a result, since 1983, he has grown Costco into a $116 billion giant.

I wanted to hear from him personally about how difficult this has been. In our most recent conversation, during the summer of 2016, he was at his home in Napa Valley, where he owns an award-winning winery, managed by his son. He began the conversation by quoting from an old article about Costco that contained a line probably meant as criticism, but which has become a badge of honor he proudly repeats — even though it isn't entirely accurate. What's true is the *spirit* of the statement: put customers and employees first, and shareholders will reap rewards naturally. In Jim's words: "We had someone who wrote a major piece on us with a phrase that caught on. What he concluded was, it was better to be a Costco employee and a Costco customer than to be a Costco shareholder. In the early days, we had critics who would come in here, look at what we were doing, and say, 'You're charging $74.99 for that bottle of wine? You could easily get $90 for it.' They had the same reaction to our wages and health care."

In other words, people thought he was a little crazy. When he founded the company, it was a struggle simply getting a license to run his original warehouse club in the state of Washington. Nothing made sense to the state officials who peppered him with queries about how he was going to make it work. They all suspected he would be cutting corners, cheating somebody somewhere — because they couldn't see how you could charge a customer to shop in a warehouse. Who would pay a store to shop there? Why would people flock to a place with a smaller than usual selection of products, many of them stacked to the ceiling, while forklifts shuttled inventory around through the aisles at all hours? It sounded bizarre: something had to be amiss.

So Jim and his team realized they needed to become a model of virtue — to prove they were on the level with their business model. They vowed to be impeccable and unimpeachable: "We sat down and decided we were going to overcome any objection anyone would have to shopping with us. We would offer a full customer-satisfaction warranty for the membership as a whole. We would have the best refund policy, not only for the products, but also for the membership fee. If people were unhappy at any point in time, we gave them back their fee. We'd have no superlatives in advertising. Put the stuff out there and let the customer make the choice. Never carry a second or irregular. No one would be able to say we were making money off the backs of our employees, because we'd have the best wages and best benefit plan. It was all part of establishing our four fundamental principles, our code of ethics."

As a result, membership grew and has never stopped growing, as have sales, and shareholders have seen even more amazing returns than anyone might have expected.

"Our sales have compounded since 1985 at about 13 percent per year. Our earnings are pretty much the same: 13.2 [percent]. Our stock has grown at 16.1 percent."

"Sixteen percent? That's incredible, Jim," I said.

"We were resolute in what we believed. It's a pretty simple story. We did it by being consistent. We have the best prices around. We have the best value around. It's tough *not* to do business with us, unless you ignore the value proposition. Generally speaking, people will see what you're doing and talk about it. Word of mouth is the most significant form of advertising. It's better to have someone else saying something nice about you than to be doing it yourself. People say, 'You guys are the conversation at cocktail parties. Somebody is always saying you had a pumpkin pie for $5.95 or a Coach handbag for $250 that someone knows sells for $450 somewhere else.'"

It wasn't always easy. Some quarters and some years were rough, and the activists would pounce. But Sinegal and his team held fast to their core principles by stressing that they were in the business for the long term, not for quarterly results.

"The temptation is to slide the prices up and decrease the value equation. That must have been intense," I said.

"That's the history of the retail business. When I was a boy, Sears and Roebuck was the Costco of the land. All of America shopped there. Great value. Great quality. Look at them today."

"They violated every single one of your principles. They violated all four of them," I said.

"They have become irrelevant."

Behind the four principles, though — and what enables Costco to stay true to them — is a fanatical devotion to efficiencies in their business model: keeping all costs other than labor as low as absolutely possible.

"I remember sitting down with a top executive from P&G fifteen, twenty years ago, and we were having a glass of wine, and he took a cocktail napkin and started calling some numbers, comparing SG&A [selling, general, and administrative costs] for various companies. He says, you look at Walmart, which has an SG&A of 15 percent, and Target has an SG&A of 21 percent, and Kmart has a 24 or 25, and Sears has a 32 percent SG&A . . . You don't have to be a Rhodes scholar to know who is going to win this game."

I asked, "What was yours over the years?"

"Less than ten. Fractionally under ten."

In those six words you have the fulcrum of his success. He gave himself the freedom to be good to his employees, his customers, and his suppliers because his business had performed at an Olympic level in terms of day-to-day and month-to-month operations. Costco keeps finding every last way to cut waste and lower costs to a level unheard of in its industry — without cutting wages or laying people off. It has turned retail into a constantly refined art form. Why? To nourish its lifeblood: the customer and the employee. Rigorous, systematic efficiencies from top to bottom give Costco the freedom to treat their employees as human beings, not simply as resources or costs.

But note something else in those words. Jim quickly modified his "less than ten" into "fractionally under ten." In that little throwaway self-correction, I could hear something at the heart of those four rules of his — and that was decency, honesty, and integrity. He wanted to be absolutely clear about that tenth of a percent; to not make it sound as though his company had achieved more than it actually had. This was humbling evidence of what's really at work in a great company: the goodness and humanity of its leadership. Absolute honesty and this kind of scrupulous care with the fractional numbers is what makes everything else I'm talking about in this book possible — clear-eyed candor about the pivotal role of performance or the lack of it.

I told him, "Ken and I have been talking with CEOs, and they say basically, 'Yeah, the problem of inequality of opportunity is serious and the consequences that are separating America into haves and have less, yeah we get that . . . But what do you expect me to do? The market will go after me.'"

"Activists are the greediest people on the planet," Jim said without a pause. "They may try to BS that their interest is with the shareholders, but it's all about greed with them. How do you explain what happened in 2008 other than greed? However, be forewarned. The courts will take the side of the shareholder every time. If you can't produce, they're going to drum you out of the corp. You will lose your company. You either go along, or you are gone."

"Agreed," I said. "But let's go back to Jim Sinegal in 1983. As you went along, the same thing happened. Razor-thin margins and all these guys crying wolf. But you, with the lowest margins, managed to create a business model that worked with those margins and did better for shareholders than most. A 16 percent compounded rate of return to shareholders is unbelievable."

"What if I told you," Jim said, "that in the expense of running our company, 70 cents of every dollar we spend is spent on people? Clearly that is the major ratio you have to look at in any company. If you get into trouble, and you are pressured, where are you going to look first? If you have any brains at all, that will be the first place. Labor. The second place is, how can I take this item that I'm charging $29 for and get $32 for it? That is essentially what happens. And it's the wrong tactic, in both cases."

"I remember the big supermarkets used to be A&P. And Ames."

"Ames. In 1980, they were bigger than Walmart. Where are they now? You have to decide what you want to be. We are in an industry, and I'm sure there are others as well, where we can point to all these stories of failures and say look what happened. That's the history, the evolution of this business; if you want to survive, you pay attention to the core principles. You don't have a choice. That leads us back to the whole crux of the matter. From the very beginning, we were not going to take a short-term view of our business. We wanted to be here fifty years from now. When you take that view, you do things differently. One bad quarter doesn't determine whether you're a good or bad company. In our company we were all reading from the same sheet of music. That's what matters."

"It's a fantastic story," I said. "Your principles can apply to anything, from a Google to McKinsey & Company."

"It can happen in any industry. You have to perform — at all levels. The customers vote at the checkout stand or on the orders. No matter what the business is. Sticking to the fundamental principles is how you get that vote."

COSTCO IS ONLY ONE AMONG MANY

Some other remarkable companies already embody this new paradigm. They operate with *all* stakeholders in mind, pay their workers well, and balance the need for annual profit against a concern for investing sufficiently in the company's future. Google, Qualcomm, Home Depot, Adobe, and Autodesk are just a few of the firms recognized for their management, and they are often in *Fortune*'s list of the one hundred best companies to work for. They are judged on a number of criteria, but most crucially, all of them are also in the list of organizations that pay their people exceptionally well.

Google represents the best poster child as a twenty-first century enterprise. It is an organization totally committed to sustained innovation. It has an enlightened management that invests generously in two areas: creativity/innovation and employees. It hires the most creative people it can find, but it also rewards them and recognizes them as the firm's greatest asset. Google pays its people more than any other company in the tech world and has embraced values that guard a supportive, fun, and inventive environment. Yet along with these ample rewards comes a demand for excellence and superior performance. It's a magic formula with proven results in the marketplace.

Average annual income for an hourly worker at Qualcomm is $64,792. The company also has awarded a $1,500 bonus to each of the 1,794 employees who have filed new patents. In other words, they are intensely focused on two things: fair compensation and innovation. The two are inextricably linked. Happy employees are more inventive and motivated than unhappy ones. With an employment of 17,731, Qualcomm created an astonishing 2,482 new jobs in 2015.

EMPLOYEES CAN BE SHAREHOLDERS

Publix, a regional supermarket chain, also puts the employee first. Publix serves customers in Florida. Nearly every worker you encounter will ask you what you need, escort you to the aisle where it's located, and offer to do nearly anything to make your experience more pleasant or fruitful than it was a minute before they met you. In the case of Publix, this kind of exceptional customer service grows out of a sense of ownership through its Employee Stock Ownership Plan (ESOP). With this company, the employees don't just take ownership of their job responsibilities, they actually own the company. *Forbes* summarized it:

All staffers who have put in 1,000 work hours and a year of employment receive an additional 8.5% of their total pay in the form of Publix stock. (Though private, the board sets the stock price every quarter based on an independent valuation; it's pegged at $26.90 now, up nearly 20% already this year.) How rich can employees get? According to Publix, a store manager who has worked at the company for twenty years and earns between $100,000 and $130,000 likely has $300,000 in stock and has received another $30,000 in dividends. [A worker's] rate of ownership is based on ... wages. This encourages the hardest workers . . . giving them a real stake in the company as they labor.[1]

These policies leapfrog over the obsession with short-term shareholder value. Employees need both a continuing salary and a share of the additional profit that derives from their efforts to treat customers like family. If everyone is making the bulk of his or her living at a company, and also owns a piece of it, they won't choose to do anything that would boost share price while also hurting the longevity of the firm. In 2015, Publix was hailed by *Forbes* as the most profitable grocer in the United States, with net profit margins of 5.6 percent in 2012. Those are considerably higher than the industry standard. Yet Publix pays its salaried store managers a remarkable average of $115,000 per year. *Forbes* quoted Publix CEO Ed Crenshaw last year: "I'm always amazed that more companies don't recognize the power of associate ownership."[2]

Southwest Airlines remains one of the most remarkable success stories in American business over the past quarter century. After its first year as a start-up, Southwest has been profitable for thirty-nine consecutive years. It has consistently ranked high in *Fortune*'s list. Like Publix, Southwest has given its employees a stake in the company itself.

At any given time, Southwest employees own as much as 15 percent of the company. Colleen Barrett, president emeritus and company cofounder along with Herb Kelleher, says, "Employees feel like owners because they are owners. We've had flight attendants and mechanics leave Southwest as millionaires. We treat them like family."[3] To understand how Southwest's management principles could be a bellwether of one powerful initiative to narrow the income gap in this country, we turn to a story in the *New York Times* from 2006. In it, a man who collects boarding passes — now a millionaire on the strength of his company stock — is still working for Southwest, having joined the company when it was founded in the early 1970s. He doesn't need the income, so why's he staying in his seat? He loves the company and wants to be a part of whatever happens next.[4]

In business today, the maximization of shareholder value skews unreasonably to a privileged few. It's not only morally perverse, but it also robs the business of its greater potential and contributes to income inequity. Southwest has broadened its ownership to channel the rewards of success to everyone who has helped make it happen.

PAY WELL FOR EMPLOYEE DEVOTION

When you look at tech companies, the picture is even more generous. Adobe Systems pays an average salary of $134,630, and its hourly workers bring in a startling $88,108. Going down the line with these leading companies, you can see the same picture: management that understands how happy employees make for a creative, energized workplace, and, ultimately, happy and loyal customers.

Years ago, Henry Ford provided one of the best examples of a CEO recognizing the core significance of the average worker in a free-enterprise economy. It was really simple common sense, but such a move was unprecedented. Without being pressured to do it, from inside or outside his company, he doubled his workers' wages. This created a happy, loyal, and diligent workforce. It also, secondarily, created a market for his product. On a macro scale, it boosted the growth of a middle class, forming a market that went on to support his business for decades. Ford's website describes his radical gesture in a nutshell:

> In 1914, Henry Ford started an industrial revolution by more than doubling wages to $5 a day—a move that helped build the U.S. middle class and the modern economy. The pay

increase would also be accompanied by a shorter workday (from nine to eight hours). While this rate didn't automatically apply to every worker, it more than doubled the average autoworker's wage. Newspapers from all over the world reported the story as an extraordinary gesture of goodwill.[5]

It was much more than that. It was enlightened free-market capitalism. As CEOs reconsider compensation for the general workforce, they need to take a clear look at their own compensation. Few people are going to be willing to work for a single dollar, as John Mackey does at Whole Foods, but top management needs to reign in the widening ratio between the annual earnings at the top and the average worker's wage. Most of the time, lavish CEO pay packages have little or nothing to do with actual performance; rather, the rewards are tied to stock price and total shareholder return, which are too often financially engineered. As we move away from shareholder primacy, the evaluation criteria will move more toward value creation as a measure of performance. Over time, CEO compensation needs to become less extreme and much more tied to stakeholder value based on long-term growth, fairer compensation for employees, and measures of a brand's actual worth in the market. Financial engineering must recede. Boards of directors must take the lead in this important but essential transition.

ENLIGHTENED MANAGEMENT IS MORE PROFITABLE

One may legitimately ask whether these "experiments" in a new interpretation of free-market capitalism actually work. Well, data demonstrates that these pioneer companies do just that. A remarkable book, *Firms of Endearment: How World-Class Companies Profit from Passion and Purpose*, tracks forty corporations that focus on all levels of "value" — emotional, experiential, social, and financial. These companies (referred to as FOEs) serve all stakeholders, and their overall returns, outlined in the table below, show how their shareholders have been rewarded even more generously than those of companies focused on shareholder primacy.

**Annualized returns for firms of endearment,
October 1998–September 2013[5]**

Annualized Performance	15 years	10 years	5 years
US FOEs	21.17%	17.69%	20.24%
Internal FOEs	18.53%	19.86%	20.46%
S&P 500	5.32%	7.55%	9.98%

Common sense can guide us in understanding how this works. More motivated employees, backed by higher investment in the long-term future, produce greater profits and happier stakeholders. The purpose of business isn't simply shareholder value, *by any means*: it's a matrix of outcomes, not only for owners and shareholders, but also for employees, customers, communities, and the environment. A company has to benefit everything and everyone it touches. First and foremost are its employees. Their lives depend on being able to earn a fair wage, and our economy depends on their ability to keep earning those wages.

EMPLOYEES AND CUSTOMERS TO THE RESCUE

A few years ago, a quiet private-sector revolution took place in Boston. Yes, it involved only one company, an outlier, yet it's an exception that ought to become the rule.

Market Basket, a fine grocery retailer, has stores in the Boston area and parts of New Hampshire. The company is family owned, extremely successful, and quite profitable. The ownership was divided among family members, including the CEO and five others. Disagreements grew heated between two camps that split the family apart. All five of the other family members teamed up with a consultant to argue against the CEO on several points:

- The company was buying only top-quality produce. If they lowered standards a tier or two, they could cut costs in ways that customers wouldn't notice.

- Employee salaries were too high. They wanted to reduce pay scales and benefits when hiring capable replacements.

- The company employed more people than it needed on the floor. Competitors didn't feel the need to have as many people to help customers navigate the aisles.

There were a number of other issues as well, all directed toward boosting profit by lowering quality of service.

The CEO refused to accept these suggested measures. He argued that none of them could be implemented without harming service and the quality of products customers knew they could find at Market Basket. As a result, the CEO was voted out — fired by the other insurgent family members.

This assault on the culture that the CEO had spent many years building gave rise to a startling, friendly uprising. The established employees, who were also fired or knew they were about to be let go, began picketing the stores. What happened next was virtually unique: customers joined them in the picket lines. Not only that, many of these customers began shopping at competitive supermarkets and then defiantly taping their grocery receipts to the windows of their favorite Market Basket store. Within a few weeks, the company was bleeding cash. The governors of Massachusetts and New Hampshire anticipated where all this would lead. They had no desire to see Market Basket fall into bankruptcy, with thousands of employees left unemployed. So they stepped in to help negotiate a settlement. The CEO's faction within the family bought out the dissident shareholders, and the company returned to normal — albeit with debt it must now work off.

The result: all the loyal customers came rushing back, followed by new customers who had read about this remarkable intramural battle on their behalf. Employees hailed the CEO as a hero and doubled their daily devotion to customer satisfaction.

It's almost a parable of how business can, and should, be run — and why it works. It's about human relationships — between management and workers, as well as a company and its employees. Shareholders who lose sight of that primary truth, as so many have been doing over the past four decades, risk everything in the pursuit of easy profit. The role of business isn't simply to maximize short-term profits on the backs of employees and customers. Too many corporations have forgotten how the Golden Rule essentially serves as the core value at the most enlightened companies: doing the right thing for others eventually brings sustainable growth and profitability.

A NEW METRIC: EMPLOYEE MILEAGE

Nowhere has the practice of long-term care and respect for employees reaped more impressive rewards than at Home Depot. From the first day it opened for business, it created a sound foundation in its focus on employees. Founders Bernie Marcus and Arthur Blank, along with their visionary angel investor — my friend Ken Langone — understood just how crucial the Home Depot associate would be to their success.

Nearly a year after Ken and I had our inaugural breakfast and hit the road with our plea to the private sector, we found ourselves back in Florida together this past winter. We talk all the time by phone, but this was a good chance to sit down in a relaxed environment and compare notes. I asked Ken to tell me in more detail about a set of performance measures he'd spoken about in the past. He called them his "mileage charts." In reality, they are an unprepossessing set of numbers that most financial analysts would probably never see — or care about, for that matter. They measure how long Home Depot people stay employed at the company.

This isn't a metric you hear much about. Why? It has little or nothing to do with short-term profit. However, it has everything to do with the long-term viability of American free enterprise. So, of course, it isn't something most business leaders would cite as a measure of their impact on the company, since most of them are thinking primarily about the next quarter. Yet, these numbers are Ken's holy grail. (He isn't involved anymore in the operation of Home Depot, but he's as obsessively informed about it as most people would be with a son or daughter or grandchild. It's still his baby.)

"Tell me about that chart you love, Ken," I said. "What exactly are you tracking with it?"

"The mileage chart?"

"Yes, that's it."

"It shows longevity of our employees by position: manager, assistant store manager, department head, and associate. Here are the longevity numbers. In 2007, the average longevity of an associate was 4.5 years. For a part-timer, 2.6 years. Now, the longevity for a full-timer is 8.4 years. And part-time has risen to 2.74 years. Total retail hourly workers went from 3.76 years in 2007 to 5.27 years now. Here is where you really see the numbers. A department supervisor in '07 was 5.06 years and today is 8.07 years. Our district managers stuck around for 12.28 years in '07. Now they stay at Home Depot for an average of 16.86 years."

"That's a testimony to how it's working. They don't want to leave," I said.

"The longer you can keep your people," he said, "the better your safety issues are. You don't have to retrain people. Same with entry-level hourly associates. Their experience and knowledge don't go back to zero because you had to hire somebody else. There are multiple ways that this reduces costs and increases the effectiveness of everyone employed at the stores."

What the mileage chart really shows is that people who work at Home Depot are constantly becoming more and more loyal to the company and are essentially turning themselves into a living repository of expertise — which is there for every customer to tap. Many of these people come in with a high-level skill set to begin with, as well. Tradespeople, plumbers, and electricians join Home Depot at higher wage scales and are able to solve problems for customers from day one. It pays to incentivize them to stick around, keep learning, and know the store inside and out. There is no substitute for the wisdom that comes from longevity on the floor at Home Depot: associates become master problem solvers.

I asked Ken how Home Depot is continuously intensifying this loyalty — i.e., longevity.

"From the day we started the company, we never paid minimum wage, always a buck an hour or so more than minimum. We always structured compensation so that the better you perform in the store, the more you would be rewarded. We have people in our stores making $22, $23, $24 an hour. Many have special skills, but even [for those] with no skills, we have a career path for kids who come in that lets them rise to whatever level they can achieve. The real entry level is the lot person. The one who pushes the carts back from the far end of the lot or helps customers load up. We have people who started in the parking lot; when minimum wage was $8, they were making $10 an hour. A few of those original lot people are now multimillionaires. We have a variety of different ways they can participate in an ownership capacity."

"Tell me more about that."

"Every store has a goal. If that store exceeds its goal, each associate gets a bonus. That bonus is paid out twice a year. It's reset every six months. It's possible a store will not make its revenue target, but there will be some percentage of success. Assuming you come within a certain percentage of your plan, you get some measure of success. If you exceed target, you get extra. You can tell when we send out those checks just by walking around the store — you can see it in their faces, the attitude of the people. That compensation really matters. What a boost for morale and dedication. And there's a future; you can keep moving up. There really is opportunity. For instance, right now the African American woman at the corporate level who oversees all 2,300 stores started out as an assistant cashier. She is doing an absolutely spectacular job. She is making well into the seven figures. This system works. We know it works."

"The crux of it all is what happens out on the floor, right?" I asked.

"We insist our store managers spend as little time in their offices as possible and as much time as they can on the floor — with employees and customers," Ken said. "The thing that matters almost as much as the money is recognition. Knowing someone by name. I told the store managers, if I came into the store and lined up all your associates without their aprons — without their name tags — would you know their first name? If not, shame on you. We don't just emphasize the money; we reflect on the person as a person. We have a robust system for making sure everyone has a chance for promotion."

"The practical reality of what you do is fairly simple: it's how you respect them and pay them," I said. "The results are terrific.

So what the heck is going on where the other guys are saying, 'I'll pay as little as I can and I'm not going to reward people'? The stupidity of it! We are creating a huge problem in our country with a system that doesn't work. Meanwhile, look at how Home Depot is thriving."

Ken summed it up: "It's the impact of management. The people who don't understand the importance of taking care of their employees will achieve only very short-term results. They won't have the staying power of a Costco or a Home Depot or a Google or these other companies that are doing it the right way. People are hired at the store level, and we have only one corporate rule: pay them what they're worth."

"You respect them and reward them, and they stick around and produce," I said. "It's seems pretty obvious, doesn't it?"

And, again, here is where Ken showed what lies at the core of such an enlightened system of management: an inescapable compassion for other people, even the ones who aren't lucky enough, or educated enough, to land a job at Home Depot. He isn't just concerned about how the company treats its employees. It breaks his heart to think of what might happen to the ones that Home Depot turns away. He kept talking about them even though we had actually finished our conversation.

"Think of the rigorous process when we hire, Peter," he said. "The tests they take. What about the ones who don't get a job? The ones who can't read and write or count. They come out of school that way now. What happens to them? We'll take care of the ones who stick with us. What about the ones who don't make the cut?"

If we had more people like Ken Langone putting his two cents into the business model for every new enterprise in America, this country would be in a completely different place. Yes, making your customers and employees your first consideration, in all things, is the way to make far more profit in the long run, but there's more to it than that: it's profitable because it's good, and people are drawn to what's good. As Ken pointed out, you can see it in the faces of all the associates at Home Depot. They know they are valued and respected and honored as the foundation of the company's success. Any customer who walks through the door will feel that with every encounter on the floor — and it's irresistible.

As I listened to Ken talking, I also kept hearing Jim Burke years ago, teaching the J&J credo: "Respect the employees, pay them fairly, treat them with dignity." Yes, it's a way of going back to the future. The great companies always have won with these basic values. Burke, Sinegal, Langone, and a long roll call of others: they all found the answer in the *real* value creators — the employees.

More and more often, the only way to establish a competitive edge now is by recognizing employees as the ultimate source of success, not just a company's largest expense. Loyal employees beget loyal customers, and success for any company now pivots on that loyalty. A CEO who operates by the most humane values will find that his or her workers will do nearly anything to make sure their company succeeds. And customers will gravitate to that kind of purpose and energy.

BUSINESS LEADS, GOVERNMENT FOLLOWS

As business commits itself to a new focus on its workforce, government will eventually need to follow its example. Public pressure and business success will inevitably lead government to act. But a partnership will demand that government provide business with an environment conducive to investment and risk taking. Clear, predictable, sustained rules are essential. For business to invest more generously in its workforce, it needs to trust that government won't undercut its wager on the future. Regulations must have a clear purpose and remain consistent. Continuous government interference and changes in the rules of the game inspire only risk-averse behavior in the private sector. The right environment creates a stable and predictable set of rules well into the foreseeable future.

Together, government and the private sector can turn the economy around in remarkable ways. As we pointed out earlier, major innovations in America's past depended on exactly this kind of partnership: NASA, the Human Genome Project, the Internet — these are the sorts of projects that could take shape again. Today, people are angry; business and government don't have a mutually respectful relationship. The system isn't working. Business leaders can begin to turn that around. Collaboration between the public and private sectors can help build greater and greater trust and team-work and more positive outcomes in the marketplace.

Why should we continue to support a failing and destructive sys-tem of free enterprise when better, more enlightened approaches can produce superior results? Simply, we should evolve away from shareholder primacy. That paradigm will change eventually, out of necessity — when we have no choice. But why not choose to run a company in a way that is demonstrably better right now?

Those whom the current system is failing are making them-selves known and heard politically. Donald Trump and Bernie Sanders rode a wave of revulsion over what has happened to cap-italism in this country. Isn't it the perfect time to change it — in ways that are already proving themselves in the lives of employees and in returns to shareholders?

8.

THE TIME TO ACT IS NOW

FACED WITH ALL THIS, Ken and I talked about what we could and couldn't do to raise awareness among key influencers in the private sector. For months we met with CEOs, think tanks, non-profits, foundations, and other individuals and organizations, and we found common ground in many places. Yet we wanted to jump-start the process a bit — scale it up somehow. We needed to ring the bell — to call attention to the issue and ignite constructive conversation about it.

We decided to do an op-ed, which is easy enough to write (if you know what you need to say, and we did) but hard to get published. We made a list of potential news organizations and decided there were only four viable choices: the *New York Times*, the *Wall Street Journal*, the *Washington Post*, and the *Financial Times*. We started with the *New York Times*. At least I knew where to send the story. I'd been submitting pieces for months on various subjects, to no avail, but I'd always gotten a polite and brief decline. Luckily, this one caught the eye of an editor, and a long back and forth of revisions ensued until we'd polished it enough to pass muster. I was told early, a week before the publication date, that it would appear on August 9, 2015, in that Sunday's "Week in Review." It would go online at the *Times*'s digital site two days earlier. But first we faced a gauntlet: the fact-checkers.

I got a call with a list of issues — claims we'd made and data cited that required verification and support. I quickly fired back an e-mail with answers to all but one issue. It had to do with the chart on consumption data — similar to what we show in figure 1. I mentioned that I hadn't done the analysis myself, but my economist,

Andrew Terrell, had produced the numbers in Washington DC, by using various governmental labor statistics. I clicked "send" and figured we were all set.

Around 10:30 that night, I got a call from Andrew. He mentioned the name of the woman who was doing the fact-checking, and he said she had contacted him directly and wanted to know the exact pages we'd relied on in the Labor Bureau's documentation.

"She wants to see the actual sheets of paper, I think," Andrew laughed. "I didn't know newspapers did this."

I hadn't even given the fact-checker any information about Andrew other than his name: no phone, no address, not even where he worked. The *Times* knew how to verify data, and they did.

When the op-ed appeared, first online and then on Sunday, the headline read "Capitalists, Arise." It laid out, very briefly, the vision of our economy that I'm presenting in far more detail here. Critically, it called upon the business community to join this movement. We asked for higher wages across the board for all employees other than top managers, as well as increased reinvestment in R&D. From whence all this money? It could be diverted from dividends and stock buybacks. We told of the potentially disastrous consequences of doing nothing. We wanted all business people, all fellow capitalists, to act and change business culture with a new alignment toward all stakeholders, not just shareholders. We urged action now. Immediately.

Minutes later, the groundswell of response began. Hundreds of comments appeared in the first few hours of publication, under the online version, and hundreds more kept coming. I was told it was one of the most e-mailed op-eds that week. Within the first day after publication, more than a thousand comments had been posted. Within days the number approached several thousand. The paper's editors, seeing that we'd hit a nerve, contacted me and asked me to submit written answers to a dozen of the questions readers had submitted — they selected the questions. The comments continued to come in, and the *Times* decided to shut the gate and close the comment section. Suffice it to say, the bell had been rung.

After the *New York Times* op-ed appeared, I began to hear from many people. I immediately received two invitations to speak to important committees at the Conference Board, an organization committed to identifying critical issues confronting business in order to help develop policies that can help companies address major challenges in the market. I was delighted to appear before its policy committee. The attendees represented strategy, policy, and public-affairs leaders in corporate America, all reporting directly to their CEOs. This, I thought, would be my first chance to make an impact with the vision outlined in this book: to reach those who have the power to make decisions in the most influential American corporations. I was a bit apprehensive.

At the same time, I was eager to find out what areas of push-back I might encounter. We would be better prepared to discuss issues with the CEOs after I'd had this chance to warm up, as it were, with their direct reports.

I spoke with them for just under an hour. At the end, I was completely taken aback. Their reaction was overwhelmingly positive. The people in the room not only grasped the nature of the problem (though some were startled at the seriousness of many issues), they agreed that business must respond with urgency. I was elated. Following the meeting, the group's leader wrote to me to say that this was the finest, most productive presentation he had seen in a decade of organizing these meetings.

Some weeks later, my appearance before the governance committee yielded similar results. Of course, I was mildly euphoric over what seemed to be such easy progress. But my confidence was short lived. I realized there was a major disconnect. These wonderful executives were dealing with cold, hard facts, which enabled them to realize they needed to act now and act quickly back in their own organizations. But actually taking action once they got back was another matter.

Yet, as the weeks and months followed, Ken and I logged many hours with individual CEOs, discussing in greater detail what might be done. And after each of these conversations, the outcomes began to appear disappointingly consistent: agreement on the problem, agreement on the solutions, and agreement on the potentially disastrous consequences if nothing is done. But most concluded there was nothing they could do on their own. Across the board, they concluded that it was too risky for them as individuals.

It might be the best thing for their companies in the long term, but not in the short term for their careers. This was not a cold, calculated response; the emotional struggle involved in their dilemma was palpable and genuine. Shareholder activists would descend and have their heads. The short term was all that mattered.

So eventually, I was faced with the pushback I'd anticipated — like the roadblocks I'd encountered with Jerry Bauer. He and the others haven't ruled out making changes, but they are simply hesitant to act alone. CEOs are on the hot seat. They need the cover of group consensus — a coalition of other leaders who would act in concert to provide safety in numbers.

This was a profound insight for Ken and me. We realized we need to address groups of CEOs together and boards of directors assembled into a single audience. We need to bring the media around to begin talking about this shift from short-term profit to long-term growth. We need to engage the equity holders (institutions, most of all) to support the companies that embark on the longer-term vision together with a commitment to optimize the interests of all stakeholders. We need to celebrate the early adopters, the leaders and the companies who have already been doing what we've been preaching for many years now. The ones who buck the conventional wisdom and the destructive culture of shareholder primacy. Their companies are not only surviving; they are thriving. In the fall of 2016, Ken and I appeared before a gathering of eighty directors, sponsored by the *Financial Times*. At that session, the two of us made the case against shareholder primacy and pleaded for serious consideration of reimagining free-market capitalism to optimize benefits for all critical stakeholders, not simply shareholders. The audience responded in a way that was very encouraging: they begged us to keep telling this story to more and more audiences of boards of directors and CEOs.

But once the concerned CEOs calmed down, we were at least able to outline just what was entailed by moving forward. That's when we began to get a more willing engagement with what we were suggesting — but only in early, tentative steps.

We can preserve free enterprise, but only by moving away from shareholder primacy. It's the job not only of the CEO but also of the boards of directors, equity holders, pension funds, enlightened labor leaders, and the media. The future will grow from creativity and innovation; that will drive business. Who provides that? Employees. You see how this is beginning to add up?

I have a friend in Cleveland who, with a smile, told me this story. Last year his smallish private company doubled its earnings. They had a couple of men who were watching a vat turning slowly, and they realized that if it turned at a different speed, everything changed in the process, lowering costs and increasing yields. Their little insight doubled the company's earnings. Two humble employees created a new future for everyone in that place.

Creative insight rarely flows down from the office of the CEO. It rises up from the factory floor, the cubicle warren, and the street. Main Street. Not Wall Street.

***

Once again, here's the new paradigm: invest in creativity and innovation — which means investing in people. Hold management accountable for long-term plans and milestones. Hold management accountable for measuring the strength and value of brands. (I have metrics to do this in a very precise way, the Brand Asset Valuator. We invented and perfected that measuring system at Y&R while I was CEO.) Invest in brand building, which means investing in true value and in passing that value along to custom ers, employees, and shareholders. Invest in R&D, new businesses, and new jobs; innovations around new technology; expansion into global markets.

This new paradigm — which in many ways isn't new at all — is an appeal for CEOs to get smart about long-term profit. It's a plea for them, essentially, to think on behalf of a shareholder's long-term interests. It's a way to create what was once celebrated as a blue-chip stock, a company in which you invest and then forget about it for twenty or thirty years. It's a call to CEOs to become the sort of leaders Warren Buffett has sought out for his entire investment career. CEOs and directors looking for cover could point out all of this to shareholder activists, and anyone else looking for a quicker buck.

The book *Firms of Endearment* shows, in no uncertain terms, how enlightened management brings reliable, higher results to all stakeholders, *including shareholders*. By all measures, companies that treat employees as the core of a company's competency return far greater profits: Google, Publix, Costco, Starbucks, Home Depot, Wegmans, and Adobe. As we've shown, some of these companies have been doing this for many years. These businesses aren't just green shoots of a new order. They are firmly established.

To help, we need longer-term public/private partnerships to encourage job creation, improve education, ensure that education starts early for everyone, and rebuild our trade-school-system — to provide the right training for new types of jobs and to acknowledge the earning power of the classic, fundamental trades, along with the dignity and creativity of what used to be thought of as "just" blue-collar work.

Business has always been tough and competitive. Today, it's tougher by an order of magnitude, thanks to the increasing complexities of the global economy. It won't get easier. Yet the heart of this game now is simple and clear. Perform — get results — or you become irrelevant and soon wither away. The dinosaurs who have fallen away provide an effective reminder of how market growth and profit matter: A&P, Gimbels, Gulf Oil, Acme, Sears, Kmart, RadioShack, Kodak, and so many more.

Yet the J&J credo has endured for sixty years and is still guiding that company to success. The mantra is as simple as can be: respect and reward the customer, the employees, the corporation itself, the communities, and the suppliers; as a result, the shareholders will also reap rewards. All stakeholders are critical. By following that credo with an almost religious fervor, a company can endure the ups and downs of its industry and continue to thrive well into this or the next century.

We need leaders who also see beyond the walls of the organization. We need leaders who are committed to education for all employees and to the quality of education in their communities — because that's how we prepare people to be good, creative workers.

In summary, all American citizens need to be able to make a good life for themselves and their families. It is well worth recognizing that America is a melting pot of diverse backgrounds, races, and religions. The enlightened free enterprise of tomorrow will treat all its people with respect, fairness, and dignity, as it puts their well-being at the heart of its mission, in the interest of the enterprise as a whole.

Business has to take the lead in making this possible; if it doesn't, the consequences are devastating. What do we do first? Higher wages, more jobs, better education. The long-term reward? A return of the equal-opportunity American dream — the potential for anyone to make a better life here, which is the core hope of our culture and the ultimate justification for our free-enterprise system — *and higher sustainable profits for individual companies in the long term.*

What are the barriers to making these changes? Ignorance, arrogance, greed, lack of courage, and sometimes despair or capitulation. It's also the myth of collective security. Individual CEOs feel comfortable with the way things are because no one else is turning against the tide. They're sustaining themselves by living in denial. I think some of our leaders have actually given up on our future as a country and simply want to get the most out of the system before it falls apart. This is the most destructive attitude of all. To be fair, to hope for a better future, and to do the right thing can make you feel more vulnerable. You're stepping away from the crowd. You become an easy target when you're standing out in the open by yourself, and yet you become less of a target when you're relying on the example of companies that are implementing what this book advocates and showing amazing profits as a result. We need that kind of leadership — leaders like Ken Langone, Jim Burke, Jim Sinegal, John Mackey, Paul Polman (Unilever), Kip Tindell (The Container Store), Roger Ferguson (TIAA-CREF), Howard Schultz (Starbucks), and many more today.

We must help CEOs gain some important allies in executing these vital measures, and at the top of the list are their boards of directors. They must become supporters and advocates in this shift away from shareholder primacy toward a more enlightened free-market capitalism. The equity holders (and equity managers) must also join in. This enlightened self-interest will lead to sustainable growth and a stable socioeconomic environment, and it will be part of the CEO's mission to persuade these stakeholders to be patient for long-term returns. This is not a radical shift for equity holders: we're essentially talking about the sort of long-term leadership Warren Buffet has always sought in the companies he chooses for investment. It works, in purely capitalist terms.

Finally, the media must be recruited to support this effort. Altogether, the critically needed change in our culture and business behavior can be made to happen.

When I presented the ideas in this book to one associate, he said that the book pushes back against one of the fundamental principles of business management: you can have either higher wages or more jobs, but you can't have both. We're asking for both because you *can* have both. The notion that a company is operating on the edge of its economic resources, employing only as many people as it can afford, is bunk — especially right now. As we've pointed out, US companies have parked close to three trillion dollars overseas — cash that sits idle, mainly because it has escaped taxation this way. We proposed repatriating those funds with an attractive low tax rate. Those taxes could then be spent on infrastructure jobs as economic stimulus. All the cash that would flood back into an available position on a company's books could be used to increase wages and hire and drive R&D with alternative rates of return. Nothing should suffer in the process — there would need to be no austerity measures to produce the money for this kind of growth and revitalization *within* a company. The argument that one must choose between higher wages and hiring falls apart. And anyone paying attention to our argument should have the confidence that spending will really be a form of investment — that companies that adhere to the management paradigm that we're advocating are thriving.

We need to believe in the future, especially for business. Because only business can lead the way now: it can act immediately and decisively to preserve and protect the heart and soul of a more responsible free-market economy.

Economic inequality, which is a major factor in driving the inequality of opportunity, is the most dangerous current threat to our republic. Many other seminal issues need to be addressed in the twenty-first century — immigration, energy, sustainability, infrastructure, terrorism, and more. But none of them will matter if we don't lessen inequality. It has been said that America will never be defeated by outside forces. If we perish or lose our place in the world, it will be by our own internal unwinding.

Inequality is a cancer that has already begun to eat away at our compassion and ability to see clearly how precarious our economy has become. The comfortable assurance of making easy money at the top blinds us to the corrosion of job loss and debt throughout enormous swaths of our society. It intensifies our greed, narcissism, and hunger for power. It makes us utterly different creatures from the hopeful few who landed on our shores some three hundred years ago, wanting to simply live and worship in freedom from oppression, and those who have labored and sacrificed to usher us into the twenty-first century.

The beneficiaries of a nation truly committed to equality of opportunity will spread those benefits to other segments of our society. The early winners will certainly be those lifted from their second-class status of relative economic poverty and social isolation. But eventually everyone will win, with higher long-term growth and profit throughout the private sector. The wealthy will be assured of keeping what they have earned and can choose to pass on their wealth to their own future generations, to their philanthropies, or both. Our human history and our natures have proven that there are very few guarantees and givens in life. It is only when we choose to act in accord with our higher humanity and with compassion for others that we thrive and prosper. To get and to keep, one must be willing to give. Freedom comes with responsibility and obligations. Democracy can only exist when the common good is part of our daily bread.

For businesses, inequality represents a major threat and a huge opportunity. The imperative to act is not only morally good but also represents a choice of enlightened self-interest. Business can thrive and prosper when a healthy middle class exists — and if we don't act now, it will shrivel more and more rapidly. Today's businesses can help re-create more vibrant, healthy economic growth up and down the income strata. An enlightened free-market capitalist system is the vehicle to achieve that goal.

There is another way to look at the choices ahead of us for solving this socioeconomic crisis that weighs so heavily on our nation. Throughout this book, we have seen that a healthy private sector and a healthy society are mutually dependent. A strong, inclusive society provides the essential resources for all citizens, drives the standard of living, and creates the possibility for equal opportunity. A healthy society requires an environment in which free enterprise can thrive. At the same time, business can no longer exist in the twenty-first century *without* a thriving social order. The incredible turn in our political dynamics provides whatever evidence is needed that citizens no longer tolerate the decline of the American dream and the emergence of two separate, unequal economic tiers in which a minority thrives and the rest sink into deeper debt trying to keep up.

People are understandably angry. They have said, loud and clear, that change must and will happen. The evidence in this book shows the origin of that anguish. As free-market capitalism has been hijacked, it has increasingly served smaller and smaller segments of the population while ignoring the rest. In these pages, we have provided business with the path to reimagine a powerful economic engine that produces growth and wealth to many, not just a few. We need that inclusive, democratic capitalism back, and soon. A strong, inclusive business sector drives both a healthy economy and a vibrant society. They are not just complementary; they must be symbiotic. Such a transformation requires a change in culture, a change in board governance and equity holder attitudes, and a wake-up call to academia and business schools in particular, which must know better but at this point hide like ostriches.

Yes, there is an alternative. If business chooses to isolate itself from the needs and obligations of society, government must and will step in. That's the European model. The government dictates to business who it will hire, when it can fire, how to pay, how much severance will be in cash and benefits, how long vacations have to be, and on and on. And, of course, higher taxes. It's an incredibly inefficient system, and you can easily see its outcomes in Europe's current economic crisis. To us, it's not the option America should choose. It needs to remain the road not taken. The only alternative, which is clearly unacceptable — and ultimately impossible — is the status quo, the shareholder-primacy model. We will either give it up, or it will destroy its own host.

Our country's history is rife with struggles, revolts, and serious violence. We fought a devastating civil war. Greed and power drive us to the kind of brutality and carnage that we see reoccurring today too often in Africa and the Middle East. Our twentieth-century civil rights movement faced its own kind of cruelty. History certainly points to the possibility of a violent chapter ahead to resolve the inequality problem. But looking back at history enables us to see forward — and, we hope, the best way forward. Plutocracy must end, and democracy must reenter our lives in a meaningful way.

Thus the need for urgency. The interests of our society and those of business are totally aligned. One cannot thrive unless the other does, too. That simple equation should be a new fundamental law of economics — or at least propel us business people into action.

Solving inequality in earnest will require dramatic changes. This book attempts to spell them out. It will take vision, wisdom, creativity, patience, courage, and will to fully change our current inequalities. But we can start with urgency in the business arena. We can change the dynamic of our precarious current state. We can change the dialogue and turn the crisis into a discussion of constructive possibilities. With caring and compassion, our culture and our attitudes will shift. The good people will multiply, and their efforts will be transformational. Progress and success will beget more of the same.

Business must sense the urgency and believe in the constructive possibilities. It's up to all of us. The time for action is now.

POSTSCRIPT

WHEN I ARRIVED IN America at the age of fifteen, in some ways it was as if I'd arrived from a different planet.

Separated from my parents during World War II (my father was imprisoned by the Nazis because he had worked for an American oil company in Romania), I lived through much of the war with my grandparents in a small town in Transylvania. After the war, my grandfather was arrested and eventually murdered in prison by the Communists who infiltrated our country after the war. Shortly after that, my brother and I were also arrested and put into a hard-labor camp for nearly five years, after our parents were unable to return to Romania, when the Iron Curtain came down during one of their visits to New York. Lucky for us, we were eventually released and rejoined our parents in 1954.

The point of this story is that when I arrived in New York, I had never seen an African American or even an Asian. I had grown up among people of one race and one nationality. So all I saw around me were human beings, who seemed just like me, except for small cosmetic differences. I had also never met a person of the Jewish faith, people I was also unable to distinguish from everyone else I knew.

The bigotry that I heard around me took years for me to comprehend. At first the biases and condemnations made no sense at all. The scapegoats of these slurs were people I had gotten to know and like and seemed exactly like me — which they essentially were. What became clear to me is that you have to work hard to teach and learn racism and hatred. It isn't innate. It's cultural, which makes it no less real. Above all, it's sad and tragic.

In writing this book, I chose not to address the special, more extreme plight of the African American community. The economic tragedy of the other America we've created knows no color barriers.

In Charles Murray's classic book *Coming Apart*, he describes the two Americas, two worlds divided by class and economic privilege, which is a central outcome of the economic crisis I'm writing about here. In his case, his analysis was carried out only among whites. His point and mine are essentially the same. Like a plague, the consequences of inequality do not respect color. The poor and less educated are the ones who suffer, regardless of race.

It is also true that many people of color suffer under even worse constraints. Racism only intensifies the burden they face. But the solutions outlined here apply to all Americans. Yes, the persecution of people of color makes their economic plight even worse. Yes, the incarceration of an outsized percentage of young black males is egregious. Their hopelessness and desperation only compound their despair.

But the starting point for the vast majority of have-too-much-less Americans is in fact the same. It calls for higher wages and more jobs. Eventually, equal-quality education must become the long-term equalizer for all of our children. Much more needs to be done for all groups that have suffered the horrors of bigotry and persecution. All of us, regardless of religion, race, or sexual orientation, must learn more tolerance and compassion, love and engagement with one another.

It's my earnest hope that one day, every child will experience the same wonderment I experienced when I arrived in this country. With surprise and real interest, I saw people just like me except for a different skin tone. For all of us, that slight difference must likewise become a momentary curiosity, and nothing more.

NOTES

INTRODUCTION

1. Francesco Guerrera, "Welch Condemns Share Price Focus," *Financial Times*, March 12, 2009. https://www.ft.com/content/294ff1f2-0f27-11de-ba10-0000779fd2ac.

CHAPTER 1. CAPITALISM ON THE BRINK

1. Darryl Lorenzo Wellington, "The Twisted Business of Donating Plasma," *The Atlantic*, May 28, 2014, http://www.theatlantic.com/health/archive/2014/05/blood-money-the-twisted-business-of-donating-plasma/362012/.

CHAPTER 2. THE DANGEROUS INEQUALITY

1. Bill Gates, "Why Inequality Matters," *Gates Notes*, October 13, 2014, https://www.gatesnotes.com/books/why-inequality-matters-capital-in-21st-century-review.

2. Janet L. Yellen, "The Importance of Asset Building for Low and Middle Income Households," speech given at Assets Learning Conference of the Corporation for Enterprise Development, September 18, 2014, http://www.federalreserve.gov/newsevents/speech/yellen20140918a.htm.

3. Mark Rank, "Poverty in America Is Mainstream," *New York Times*, November 2, 2013, http://opinionator.blogs.nytimes.com/2013/11/02/poverty-in-america-is-mainstream/.

4. David Vandiver, "What Is the Great Gatsby Curve?," White House Blog, June 11, 2013, https://www.whitehouse.gov/blog/2013/06/11/what-great-gatsby-curve.

5. You can view the ad featuring Aniston at https://www.youtube.com/watch?v=FFyVSczLCig.

6. Annie Lowrey, "Study Finds Income Inequality in Nation's Thriving Cities," *New York Times*, February 20, 2014, http://www.nytimes.com/2014/02/20/business/economy/study-finds-greater-income-inequality-in-nations-thriving-cities.html.

7. Natalie Sabadish and Lawrence Mishel, "CEO Pay and the Top 1%," Economic Policy Institute, May 2, 2012, http://www.epi.org/publication/ib331-ceo-pay-top-1-percent.

CHAPTER 3. THE OUTCOME OF INEQUALITY

1. Miles Corak, "State of the Union: Economic Mobility," in *Pathways: The Poverty and Inequality Report 2016*, Stanford Center on Poverty

and Inequality, 51–57, http://inequality.stanford.edu/sites/default/files/Pathways-SOTU-2016-Economic-Mobility-3.pdf.

2. Jess Miller, "Putnam: Strongest Predictors of Happiness Are Social Relationships, *Chautauquan Daily*, July 23, 2013, https://chqdaily.wordpress.com/2013/07/23/putnam-strongest-predictors-of-happiness-are-social-relationships.

3. Harvard University, Center on the Developing Child, "Toxic Stress," accessed December 7, 2016, http://developingchild.harvard.edu/science/key-concepts/toxic-stress.

4. Dale Keiger, "Kathryn Edin Reveals the Live of People Who Live on $2 a Day," *Johns Hopkins Magazine*, Winter 2015, http://hub.jhu.edu/magazine/2015/winter/kathryn-edin-living-on-2-dollars-a-day.

5. Michelle Alexander, "Ta-Nehisi Coates's 'Between the World and Me,'" *New York Times*, August 17, 2015, http://www.nytimes.com/2015/08/17/books/review/ta-nehisi-coates-between-the-world-and-me.html.

CHAPTER 4. THE PERFECT STORM

1. Aviva Hope Rutkin, "Report Suggests Nearly Half of U.S. Jobs Are Vulnerable to Computerization," *MIT Technology Review*, September 12, 2013. https://www.technologyreview.com/s/519241/report-suggests-nearly-half-of-us-jobs-are-vulnerable-to-computerization.

2. Scott Timber, "Jaron Lanier: The Internet Destroyed the Middle Class," *Salon*, May 12, 2013, http://www.salon.com/2013/05/12/jaron_lanier_the_internet_destroyed_the_middle_class.

3. Brendan Krisel, "Nearly 60 Percent of New Yorkers Live Paycheck to Paycheck: Study," *New York City Patch*, November 27, 2016, http://patch.com/new-york/new-york-city/nearly-60-percent-new-yorkers-live-paycheck-paycheck-report.

4. Eduardo Porter, "Simple Equation: More Education = More Income," *New York Times*, September 10, 2014, http://www.nytimes.com/2014/09/11/business/economy/a-simple-equation-more-education-more-income.html.

5. Nicholas Kristof, "The American Dream Is Leaving America," *New York Times*, October 25, 2014, http://www.nytimes.com/2014/10/26/opinion/sunday/nicholas-kristof-the-american-dream-is-leaving-america.html.

6. Leslie Wayne, et al., "Leaked Documents Expose Global Companies' Secret Tax Deals in Luxembourg," The International Consortium of Investigative Journalists, November 5, 2014, https://www.icij.org/project/luxembourg-leaks/leaked-documents-expose-global-companies-secret-tax-deals-luxembourg.

7. Vlad Signorelli, *Real Clear Markets*, December 1, 2014, http://www
    .realclearmarkets.com/articles/2014/12/01/the_ferguson_story_is_
    one_about_subpar_us_growth_101406.html.

8. Steve Rattner, "Inequality, Unbelievably, Gets Worse," *New York Times*,
    November 16, 2014, http://www.nytimes.com/2014/11/17/opinion/
    inequality-unbelievably-gets-worse.html.

9. Peggy Noonan, "Trump and the Rise of the Unprotected," *Wall Street
    Journal*, February 25, 2016, http://www.wsj.com/articles/
    trump-and-the-rise-of-the-unprotected-1456448550.

CHAPTER 5. SHAREHOLDER VALUE GETS LEAN AND MEAN

1. Johnson & Johnson, "Our Credo," https://www.jnj.com/sites/default/
    files/pdf/jnj_ourcredo_english_us_8.5x11_cmyk.pdf.

2. Matthew Yglesias, "How Public Equity and Misdesigned CEO Compen-
    sation Schemes Are Killing the American Economy," *Salon*, July 26,
    2013, http://www.slate.com/blogs/moneybox/2013/07/26/profits_
    and_investment_ceo_pay_and_stock_price.html.

3. Milton Friedman, "The Social Responsibility of Business Is to Increase
    Its Profits," *New York Times Magazine*, September 13, 1970, http://
    www.colorado.edu/studentgroups/libertarians/issues/friedman-
    soc-resp-business.html.

4. Steven Pearlstein, "Social Capital, Corporate Purpose and the Revival
    of American Capitalism," Center for Effective Public Management at
    Brookings, https://www.brookings.edu/wp-content/uploads/2016/06/
    BrookingsPearlsteinv5_Revised-Feb-2014.pdf.

5. "Too Much of a Good Thing," Business in America, *The Economist*,
    March 26, 2016, http://www.economist.com/news/briefing/21695385-
    profits-are-too-high-america-needs-giant-dose-competition-too-
    much-good-thing.

6. William Lazonick, "Profits without Prosperity," *Harvard Business
    Review*, September 2014, https://hbr.org/2014/09/profits-without-
    prosperity.

7. "Too Much of a Good Thing," *The Economist*.

8. Liz Capo McCormick, "Gross Says America's Privileged 1% Should Pay
    Higher Taxes," October 31, 2013, http://www.bloomberg.com/news/
    articles/2013-10-31/gross-says-america-s-privileged-1-should-pay-
    higher-taxes.

9. See Stout's book *The Shareholder Value Myth: How Putting Sharehold-
    ers First Harms Investors, Corporations, and the Public* (Berrett-
    Koehler, 2012).

10. Matt Krantz, "Founders Make Great CEOs. Here's Why," *USA Today*,
    March 29, 2016, http://www.usatoday.com/story/money/markets/
    2016/03/28/19-companies-excel-founders-charge/82343660.

11. Gregory Watson, "Peter F. Drucker: Delivering Value to Customers," *Quality Progress,* May, 2002. http://www.gregoryhwatson.eu/ images/5-QP_Watson_-_May2002_-_Drucker_-_Delivering_Value_ to_Customers.pdf.

CHAPTER 6. THE WAY FORWARD

1. Saki Knafo, "Good Wages Are Not Enough," *The Atlantic,* June 11, 2015, http://www.theatlantic.com/business/archive/2015/06/zeynep-ton-workers-wages/395564.

2. Ibid.

3. William Galston, "The New Challenge to Market Democracies: The Political and Social Costs of Economic Stagnation," Brookings Institution, October 10, 2014, https://www.brookings.edu/research/the-new-challenge-to-market-democracies-the-political-and-social-costs-of-economic-stagnation.

CHAPTER 7. STAKEHOLDER VALUE IS ALREADY WORKING

1. Brian Solomon, "The Wal-Mart Slayer: How Publix's People-First Culture Is Winning the Grocer War," *Forbes,* August 12, 2013, http:// www.forbes.com/sites/briansolomon/2013/07/24/the-wal-mart-slayer-how-publixs-people-first-culture-is-winning-the-grocer-war/ #74275e2f7676.

2. Mary Josephs, "The Better Exit Strategy: ESOPs Satisfy Business Owners and Preserve Their Legacy," *Forbes,* February, 12, 2014, http:// www.forbes.com/sites/maryjosephs/2014/02/12/the-better-exit-strategy-esops-satisfy-business-owners-and-preserve-their-legacy/ #4858199b6892.

3. "Southwest Airlines President Emeritus Colleen Barrett on the Power of an Ownership Culture," Rady School of Management, University of California, San Diego, accessed November 27, 2016, http://rady.ucsd .edu/beyster/media/newsletter/2009/spring/Southwest.html.

4. Jeff Bailey, "On Some Flights, Millionaires Serve the Drinks," *New York Times,* May 15, 2006, http://www.nytimes.com/2006/05/15/ business/15millionaires.html.

5. Ford Motor Company, "Henry Ford's $5-a-Day Revolution," http:// ophelia.sdsu.edu:8080/ford/03-12-2011/news-center/news/press-releases/press-releases-detail/677-5-dollar-a-day.html.

6. From *Firms of Endearment: How World-Class Companies Profit from Passion and Purpose* (Upper Saddle River, NJ: Pearson Education, 2014).

BIBLIOGRAPHY

Brynjolfsson, Erik, and Andrew McAfee. *Race Against the Machine: How the Digital Revolution Is Accelerating Innovation, Driving Productivity, and Irreversibly Transforming Employment and the Economy*. Digital Frontier Press, 2012.

Durant, Will, and Ariel Durant. *The Lessons of History*. New York: Simon & Schuster, 2010. First published 1968.

Edin, Kathryn, and H. Luke Shaefer. *$2.00 a Day: Living on Almost Nothing in America*. New York: Houghton Mifflin Harcourt, 2015.

Friedman, Thomas. *The World Is Flat. New York:* Farrar, Straus & Giroux, 2005.

Lanier, Jaron. *Who Owns the Future*. New York: Simon & Schuster, 2014.

Murray, Charles. *Coming Apart, The State of White America: 1960–2010*. Reprint ed. New York: Crown Forum, 2013.

Nayar, Vineet. *Employees First, Customers Second: Turning Conventional Management Upside Down*. Boston: Harvard Business Review Press, 2010.

Piketty, Thomas. *Capital in the Twenty-First Century*. Translated by Arthur Goldhammer. Cambridge, MA: Belknap Press, 2014.

Putnam, Robert. *Bowling Alone: The Collapse and Revival of American Community*. New York: Simon & Schuster, 2001.

———. *Our Kids: The American Dream in Crisis*. Reprint ed. New York: Simon & Schuster, 2016.

Rosenbluth, Hal, and Diane McFerrin Peters. *The Customer Comes Second: Put Your People First and Watch 'em Kick Butt*. Rev. ed. New York: HarperCollins, 2002.

Sisodia, Raj, Jag N. Sheth, and David Wolfe. *Firms of Endearment: How World-Class Companies Profit from Passion and Purpose*. 2nd ed. Upper Saddle River, NJ: Pearson Education, 2014.

Stout, Lynn. *The Shareholder Value Myth: How Putting Shareholders First Harms Investors, Corporations, and the Public*. San Francisco: Berrett-Koehler, 2012.

Ton, Zeynep. *The Good Jobs Strategy: How the Smartest Companies Invest in Employees to Lower Costs and Boost Profits. New York:* Houghton Mifflin Harcourt, 2014.

ILLUSTRATION CREDITS

Figure 1. Bureau of Labor Statistics, Consumer Expenditure Survey 2014.

Figure 2. Organisation for Economic Co-operation and Development, Council of Economic Advisors (CEA).

Figures 3–5. Michael I. Norton and Dan Ariely, "Building a Better America—One Wealth Quintile at a Time," *Perspectives on Psychological Science* 6, no. 1 (January 2011): 9–12. DOI:10.1177/1745691610393524. (Copyright 2015 Peter Georgescu)

Figure 6. David H. Autor, "Skills, Education, and the Rise of Earnings Inequality among the 'Other 99 Percent,'" *Science* 344, no. 6186 (May 23, 2014): 843–51. DOI: 10.1126/science.1251868.

Figure 7. Uncertain, I think added by PG from a financial note/site.

Figure 8. Economic Policy Institute, "The Productivity-Pay Gap": EPI's analysis of data from the Bureau of Economic Analysis's National Income and Product Accounts and the Bureau of Labor Statistics's Consumer Price Indexes and Labor Productivity and Costs programs, http://www.epi.org/productivity-pay-gap/#_blank.

Figure 9. Federal Reserve Economic Data, Federal Reserve Bank of St. Louis.

Figure 10. Bureau of Economic Analysis (http://www.bea.gov/).

Figure 11. Published in *Fortune*. Sources: Organisation for Economic Co-operation and Development (OECD) and Duke University's Fuqua School of Business.

Figure 12. Ibid.

Figure 13. Analysis by GMO LLC's James Montier, including insight from New York University professor of economics John Askher et al., 2013 (https://www.gmo.com/north-america/welcome).

Figure 14. GMO and Datastream, 2014.

ACKNOWLEDGMENTS

This book became reality with the help of many, many friends and colleagues who gave of themselves selflessly to create the best version of this vital subject. To you all, thank you and bless you for your generosity.

To Ken Langone, an extraordinary businessman, philanthropist, and capitalist rebel, I thank you for your friendship, your courage, and your unfailing partnership.

To Alan Schwartz, another special friend who helped guide me onto a productive path, I am deeply indebted by your wisdom.

To Barbara Henricks, my agent, marketing pro, and good friend for more than a decade, I express my appreciation for your ideas, support, and good deeds.

I am indebted to Andrew Terrell, a brilliant young economist. A bright, exciting future awaits you. So glad our paths crossed in the making of this book.

To Jon Vegosen, loyal dedicated friend, collaborator, provider of relevant materials, and superb editor of several versions of this book. He added insights and value to our project.

Lastly, to my true partner, Dave Dorsey, at my side in writing all my three books. I am grateful for his outstanding writing, his ideas, and his steadfast support and friendship.

INDEX

 **PETER A. GEORGESCU** is chairman emeritus of Young & Rubicam, a network of preeminent commercial communications companies. He served as the company's chairman and CEO from 1994 until January 2000.

Under Mr. Georgescu's leadership, Young & Rubicam successfully transformed from a private to a publicly held company. Also during his tenure, Young & Rubicam built the most extensive database on global branding and, from its findings, developed a proprietary model for diagnosing and managing brands. Within the marketing community, Mr. Georgescu is known as a leading proponent of creating unified communications programs, agency accountability for measuring the impact of communications programs, and structuring value-based agency compensation. In recognition of his contributions to the marketing and advertising industry, Mr. Georgescu was elected to the Advertising Hall of Fame in 2001.

Mr. Georgescu immigrated to the United States in 1954 after years of forced labor as a child in communist Romania. He was educated at Phillips Exeter Academy. He received his AB with cum laude honors from Princeton and an MBA from the Stanford Business School.

Mr. Georgescu's belief in the power of education has fueled his involvement with organizations such as A Better Chance and Polytechnic University, both of which he has served as a member of their boards of directors. The University of Alabama and Cornell College in Iowa have awarded Mr. Georgescu honorary doctorate degrees. He is also the recipient of the Ellis Island Medal of Honor. In 2014, he was honored with the Spirit of New York City Award by the Cathedral of St. John the Divine.

Mr. Georgescu has also served on the boards of Levi's, Toys"R"Us, EMI Recorded Music, International Flavors & Fragrances, and Briggs & Stratton. He is currently vice chairman of New York-Presbyterian Hospital, a trustee of the Paul and Daisy Soros Fellowships for New Americans program, and a member of the Council on Foreign Relations.

He is the author of two previous books, *The Source of Success: Five Enduring Principles at the Heart of Real Leadership* (Jossey-Bass, 2005) and *The Constant Choice: An Everyday Journey From Evil Toward Good* (Greenleaf Book Group Press, 2013).

DAVID DORSEY is the author of the critically acclaimed *The Force* (Random House, 1994) and *The Cost of Living* (Viking/Penguin, 1997). *The Force* was included in *The 100 Best Business Books of All Time* (Portfolio/Penguin, 2016). Dorsey is coauthor, with Peter Georgescu, of *The Source of Success* and *The Constant Choice*. He has written for *Fast Company, Esquire, Worth,* and a variety of other publications. He lives in Pittsford, New York.

Berrett–Koehler
Publishers

Berrett-Koehler is an independent publisher dedicated to an ambitious mission: *Connecting people and ideas to create a world that works for all.*

We believe that the solutions to the world's problems will come from all of us, working at all levels: in our organizations, in our society, and in our own lives. Our BK Business books help people make their organizations more humane, democratic, diverse, and effective (we don't think there's any contradiction there). Our BK Currents books offer pathways to creating a more just, equitable, and sustainable society. Our BK Life books help people create positive change in their lives and align their personal practices with their aspirations for a better world.

All of our books are designed to bring people seeking positive change together around the ideas that empower them to see and shape the world in a new way.

And we strive to practice what we preach. At the core of our approach is Stewardship, a deep sense of responsibility to administer the company for the benefit of all of our stakeholder groups including authors, customers, employees, investors, service providers, and the communities and environment around us. Everything we do is built around this and our other key values of quality, partnership, inclusion, and sustainability.

This is why we are both a B-Corporation and a California Benefit Corporation—a certification and a for-profit legal status that require us to adhere to the highest standards for corporate, social, and environmental performance.

We are grateful to our readers, authors, and other friends of the company who consider themselves to be part of the BK Community. We hope that you, too, will join us in our mission.

A BK Currents Book

BK Currents books bring people together to advance social and economic justice, shared prosperity, sustainability, and new solutions for national and global issues. They advocate for systemic change and provide the ideas and tools to solve social problems at their root. So get to it!

To find out more, visit **www.bkconnection.com.**

Berrett–Koehler
Publishers

Connecting people and ideas
to create a world that works for all

Dear Reader,

Thank you for picking up this book and joining our worldwide community of Berrett-Koehler readers. We share ideas that bring positive change into people's lives, organizations, and society.

To welcome you, we'd like to offer you a free e-book. You can pick from among twelve of our bestselling books by entering the promotional code **BKP92E** here: http://www.bkconnection.com/welcome.

When you claim your free e-book, we'll also send you a copy of our e-newsletter, the *BK Communiqué*. Although you're free to unsubscribe, there are many benefits to sticking around. In every issue of our newsletter you'll find

- A free e-book
- Tips from famous authors
- Discounts on spotlight titles
- Hilarious insider publishing news
- A chance to win a prize for answering a riddle

Best of all, our readers tell us, "Your newsletter is the only one I actually read." So claim your gift today, and please stay in touch!

Sincerely,

Charlotte Ashlock
Steward of the BK Website

Questions? Comments? Contact me at bkcommunity@bkpub.com.

MIX
Paper from
responsible sources
FSC® C002589

Certified

Corporation
bcorporation.net